BOOK 3

READING
with
UNDERSTANDING
a comprehension course

JOHN SEELY

OXFORD UNIVERSITY PRESS 1983

Oxford University Press, Walton Street, Oxford OX2 6DP

Oxford London Glasgow
New York Toronto Melbourne Auckland
Kuala Lumpur Singapore Hong Kong Tokyo
Delhi Bombay Calcutta Madras Karachi
Nairobi Dar es Salaam Cape Town

and associated companies in
Beirut Berlin Ibadan Mexico City Nicosia

OXFORD is a trade mark of Oxford University Press

ISBN 0 19 831142 7

Also by John Seely:

Oxford Secondary English

Book 1	0 19 831133 8	Teacher's Book 1	0 19 831134 6
Book 2	0 19 831135 4	Teacher's Book 2	0 19 831136 2
Book 3	0 19 831137 0	Teacher's Book 3	0 19 831138 9

Dramakit   0 19 913238 0

Playkits   0 19 913259 3

In Context   0 19 913222 4

Typeset in Great Britain by
Rowland Phototypesetting Ltd, Bury St Edmunds, Suffolk
Printed in Great Britain by
Pitman Press Ltd, Bath

CONTENTS

ACKNOWLEDGEMENTS

The publishers would like to thank the following for permission to reprint copyright material.

Alan Blackwood: 'Professional Singer' reprinted from *The Performing World of the Singer* (1981) by permission of Breslich & Foss. **Peter Brent:** 'Fortune Telling' reprinted from *How To Tell Your Fortune* (edited by Peter Brent, 1975) by permission of Marshall Cavendish Ltd. **Victor Canning:** 'The Professor' reprinted from *The Flight of the Grey Goose* (1973) by permission of William Heinemann Ltd. **John Christopher:** 'Accident' reprinted from *Empty World* (Hamish Hamilton, 1977/Puffin Books, 1981) by kind permission of the author. **Farrukh Dhondy:** 'Go Play Butterfly' reprinted from *Come to Mecca* (1978) by permission of Collins Publishers. **Diagram Group:** 'Pencil and Paper Games' is reprinted by permission from *The Way to Play*, copyright © Diagram Group, 1975. **Peter Dickinson:** 'Buying a bike' reprinted from *Annerton Pit* (1977) by permission of Victor Gollancz Ltd. **Angus Graham:** 'The Broken Knee' reprinted from *The Golden Grindstone* (Heinemann Educational Books Ltd., 1973) by permission of A. D. Peters & Co. Ltd. **Ursula le Guin:** 'The New Car' reprinted from *A Very Long Way from Anywhere Else* (1976) by permission of Victor Gollancz Ltd. **Barbara Habenstreit:** 'The Modern City' from *Cities in the March of Civilisation* (1973) by permission of Collins Publishers. **A. L. Hendriks:** 'Jamaican Fragment' was first published in *BIM*, The Literary Magazine of Barbados, and collected in *City Stories* (Ward Lock Educational, 1979). **Barry Hines:** 'Kestrel' reprinted from *Kes* (1968) by permission of Michael Joseph Ltd. **David Hutchinson:** 'The Day After the End of the World' reprinted from *Fool's Gold* (Abelard Schuman Ltd., 1979) by permission of The Blackie Publishing Group Ltd. **Laurie Lee:** 'Bullfight' reprinted from *A Rose for Winter* (1955) by permission of the author and The Hogarth Press Ltd. **Christopher Milne:** 'The Pistol' reprinted from *The Enchanted Place* (Methuen, London, 1974) by permission of Associated Book Publishers Ltd. **Dawn Muscillo:** 'Sister Coxall's Revenge', published in *Horror* (John Murray, 1978). **Ivan Southall:** 'The Primitives' reprinted from *The Cool Man and Other Contemporary Stories by Australian Authors* (Angus & Robertson, 1973) by permission of the author. **William Trevor:** 'Charrada' reprinted from *The Children of Dynmouth* (1976) by permission of The Bodley Head. **Kurt Vonnegut:** 'Next Door' reprinted from *Welcome to the Monkey House* (1968) by permission of Jonathan Cape Ltd., on the author's behalf. **Bonnie and Paul Zindel:** 'The Audition' reprinted from *A Star for the Latecomer* (1980) by permission of The Bodley Head.

Every effort has been made to trace and contact copyright holders but this has not always been possible. We apologize for any infringement of copyright.

The publishers would like to thank the following for permission to reproduce photos:

Barnaby's Picture Library, pp.30, 70; Network, p.82; Thames Valley Police, p.47; J. Thomas, pp.24, 96; U.S. Games Systems, p.13; Western Americana, p.36.

Illustrations by: Terry Gabbey, Mozz.

1 BUYING A BIKE

Martin wants to buy a motorbike. He is going round secondhand dealers with his younger brother Jake, who is blind. They visit Joe Catch, a bike dealer in the middle of Southampton.

Section A Something wrong

In this section eight sentences have been missed out. They are printed at the end of the section in the wrong order.

☐ Work out which sentence fits which space.

☐ Write the numbers of the spaces and, against each one, put the letter of the sentence you have chosen.

He took the boys through his new-bike showroom and out by a back door into an echoing shed which smelt of dirty oil and welding gas and damp sacking, where he showed Martin a machine that made him whistle. Jake could hear the immediate note of longing that threaded through his brother's questions. The man was very very sincere, said it took a real rider to manage a beast like that – BSA Thunderbolt 850, 1964, old, yes, but sound workmanship, classic design, cheap because it's a bit more than most fellers care to handle, but you're a big guy, sir – all that. ——————— 1 ——————— Jake listened to the bellowing surge of the exhaust as he turned the throttle. The man cut the engine and waited.

'I thought I'd seen them priced a hundred quid more than that,' said Martin, half longing, half doubt.

'You're thinking of the '65 model, sir. And matter of fact if we'd got round to doing a paint job on this we'd have been asking . . .' and so on and so on, very sincere, very helpful. ——————— 2 ———————

'That's my front shop, sir,' said the man. 'My assistant's out. Mind if I leave you a minute to think it over? Start her up again if you want to – nothing wrong with that engine. But don't take her out in the yard. We're not insured for that.'

His brisk footsteps echoed away.

'If it's good as he says it's a snip,' said Martin.
——————— 3 ———————

'Supposed to do a ton and a quarter, full noise.'

'Full noise is right. You'd look pretty silly if you took it to another of your Anti-Concorde demos.'

'Bikes are different. What do you think?'

'There's something he isn't talking about.'
——————— 4 ———————

'I don't know. But he's talking so much because there's something he hopes you're not going to ask about.'

'Oh . . . sure?'

'About usual. About eighty per cent.'

'Oh . . . He looks you straight in the eyes all the time . . . Um . . . it's dead cheap, of course . . .'

'Isn't it too cheap?'

'Um . . .'

(This was quite a usual sort of conversation between the Bertold brothers. ——————— 5 ——————— It had begun with Martin as the small hero defending his blind baby brother from the dragons and ogres of the sighted world, but things had evened up since then. Nowadays Martin relied on Jake quite a bit for reading people's moods and feelings – usually their parents', but sometimes even his current girl's. And Jake had found that it was important to let Martin make his own choices and to go along with most of his wild whims; otherwise he simply became extra wild to make up for his brother's caution.)

For a while Martin hummed and grunted and clicked the big machine's controls; then he wheeled it around the shed with its coarse-tread tyres making a contented burring on the cement floor. Jake heard the back door of the shop open and close.

—————— 6 ——————

Martin grunted with the effort of lifting the monster back on to its stand. The brisk steps rang once more through the shed.

'Well, sir?' said the man, careful not to sound very interested.

'What's the frame like?' asked Martin.

'Never been in an accident, sir. One owner, never rode her flat out. —————— 7 ——————'

That's it, thought Jake. He clicked his tongue several times against his palate, a noise Mum made when Dad was telling one of his honest-to-God stories.

'Well, um . . .' said Martin, still faintly longing. 'I don't know . . . I think I'd better look around a bit more.'

'Perhaps she is a trifle too big for you, sir,' said the man.

—————— 8 ——————

'Expect so,' he said calmly. 'Anyway, I'll look around.'

No, Martin wasn't stupid.

a)   A shrill bell fizzed.
b)   'What do you mean?'
c)   Quite as good as you could hope for in a bike of that age.
d)   'He's coming back,' he whispered.
e)   'How fast will it go?' asked Jake.
f)   It took him twenty kicks to start the engine, but that was because it hadn't been run for a while.
g)   Even Martin could hear the needle under the politeness.
h)   Though Martin was almost eighteen and Jake five years younger they relied on each other a lot.

Section B   The bet

This section is divided into eight parts. The first part is printed at the beginning, but the others are printed in the wrong order.

☐ Work out what the correct order should be.

☐ Write the numbers in that order.

That eliminated both the big showrooms near the centre of South-ampton. Martin went to a phone box, consulted the yellow pages and rang half a dozen outlying shops. Only one sounded remotely hopeful. He put Jake on a bus and followed it for a mile. When Jake heard the feeble, oddly womanish double hoot of the moped's horn he got off the bus at the next stop and walked, with Martin pushing his moped beside him, down a street where he'd never been. A big blank wall caught all the noises on his left, and on the right little houses with gaps between them sent back confused replies. A strong smell of fresh timber filled the air, backed by a vaguer mixture of odours of rainy earth and old cabbage and wood-ash and manure.

1   He wobbled, steadied and wobbled again, almost falling. A woman's voice yelled at the dog just as he got the firmness of wheels beneath him, but by then he was heading straight for the echoes of the barking and there was nothing for it but to carry on with the turn – otherwise he'd have crashed straight into the factory wall. He rode back to the bike shop counting pedal-strokes so that he'd know roughly when he'd got there. He braked and felt for the road with a sliding foot.

2   'What's that?'
     'German bike. Shaft-driven, not chain. Horizontally opposed cylinders – they stick out a bit at the sides but it keeps the weight low. Very reliable. Sort of bike people use for . . . Here we are. Lovely and crummy.'
     This shed smelt of lighter grades of oil, and ancient dust, and leather and plastic. Somebody was working near door-level, making metal nudge and click.

3   It was too early in the year for flower-smells. Half way down the street bristle hissed on stone as somebody scrubbed a doorstep.
     'It feels a funny sort of area for a bike shop,' said Jake.
     'I dunno. It's poor but not a slum. Allotments and that. Quite a few people use push-bikes round here, I should think. Anyway the bloke we're going to see runs a push-bike shop and does motorbikes on the side. I don't know if I want a BMW, though.'

4   'You all right, Jake?' said Martin.
     'Fine.'
     'I thought that dog was going to have you off.'

'So did I.'

'Good,' said Mr Manayev. 'Your brother tell me you see nothing at all.'

'Not a sausage,' said Jake cheerfully.

'Then here is your bet you win. Good. Now we look at a machine, uh?'

5   He laughed at his joke but Martin took it into his head to hark back to the years of dragons and ogres.

'I bet my brother could if he had to,' he snapped.

'I bet,' said Mr Manayev.

'Do you?' said Martin.

'I say so.'

'All right,' said Jake. 'I'm not old enough to ride a motorbike, but if you'll lend me a push-bike I'll bet you ten p. I can ride it along the road and back.'

'Come then,' said Mr Manayev. 'I am not wanting anyone hurt. I am only making my joke.'

6   'I thought you said you'd bet,' said Martin, still angry.

'OK, OK,' said Mr Manayev. 'Is an old bike here, which another spill is not hurting. I set the saddle down. You sure you want that, sonny?'

'Ten p,' said Jake.

The long factory wall made it an easy road to ride in; the bike's chain was loose enough to scrape against the guard, and one pedal had a click in it, so Jake didn't need to produce his own noises to set up echoes. He'd just gone past the scrubbing sound when he heard a rush of clawed feet on tarmac and a hysterical yelping close to his left ankle.

7   'Shall not keep you three seconds,' said a man's voice from low down. 'I am Mr Manayev. And you are the young man who was ringing about one of my motorcycles, uh?'

He had a strong foreign accent and sounded elderly, irritable and suspicious. When he got to his feet Jake could tell from the level of his voice that he was very short, too.

'Aha!' he said, evidently noticing Jake's stick for the first time. 'And who of you is going to ride the machine, uh?'

☐ Read the passage and then answer the questions that follow it.

The sales ritual was the same, but very different. Mr Manayev sounded as though he hated the idea of selling his bikes and was angry with Martin for suggesting any such thing. He had three bikes in his garage, all second-hand BMWs, and Jake thought he sounded a bit nutty about them. Two of them would have cost quite a bit more than Martin could afford.

'Why don't you want so much for this one?' asked Martin. 'It's the same year.'

'Been across the Sahara is why.'

'What do you mean?'

'Been. Across. Thee. Sahara,' said Mr Manayev as if speaking to a deaf foreign idiot.

'That's what I was trying to tell you, Jake,' said Martin. 'If you want to ride a bike across the Sahara you take a BMW.'

'Naturally,' said Mr Manayev. 'So she has lived hard, but is in good nick, despite. You get three hundred mile to a pint of oil. Not bad, uh?'

The engine started second kick. Mr Manayev revved and idled it, then let Martin ride it round a bit of waste ground at the back of his yard. The engine had an odd note, not exactly muffled but not strident either.

'At least it's quieter than the other one,' said Jake when Martin came back to them.

'Which other one?' snapped Mr Manayev, bristly with suspicion.

'Oh,' said Martin casually, 'I was looking at a '64 BSA Thunderbolt up at Catch and Catch . . .'

'I know her,' said Mr Manayev with a yapping laugh. 'You not touch her, sonny. Joe Catch, he been trying to sell eight months. Frame twisted like barley sugar, uh?'

'Yes, well, I sort of thought . . .' said Martin. 'But Mr Catch swore she'd never been in a smash.'

'Correct,' said Mr Manayev. 'And why? She never been more than fifty mile an hour is why. She belong to Harry Frome, little building-man up Scarrow Road, and he puts his own side-car on her for carrying his ladders, uh? Is a good builder, but not for side-cars. How that frame is twisted!'

Jake grinned at the curious grunt by which Martin tried to suggest that this was what he'd suspected all along. Then Mr Manayev looked over the moped, which was in very good nick as it was only a year since Granpa had given it to Martin and it had been kept in a garage and serviced by Martin with detailed love. Mr Manayev got out a little book which listed dealers' prices for second-hand bikes of different makes and years and they settled on ninety-five pounds as a trade-in value for the moped.

'And two-twenty for the BMW?' said Martin.

'Two hundred,' said Mr Manayev.

'But you said . . .'

'Said is said. I was coming down to two hundred when you bargain with me. Your mother is still washing you behind the ears, uh?'

'Oh . . . thanks. What do you think, Jake?'

'OK by me.'

'Right. It's a deal.'

'Quick like that? What will you do for insurance?'

'I did the moped with my Dad's agent. We'll go back into town and fix that, then I'll pick up a helmet for Jake and the cash for you. Back about three, with luck.'

Sorting out the facts

1 How many motorbikes did Mr Manayev have?
2 One of them was cheaper than the others. Why?
3 Which bike did Martin try out?
4 How did Mr Manayev find out that Martin had been looking at another bike?
5 What did Mr Manayev say was wrong with that bike?
6 What had caused it?
7 What condition was Martin's moped in?
8 Why?
9 How much did Mr Manayev offer him for it?
10 What price did Mr Manayev finally ask for the BMW?

Understanding the story

11 What was Mr Manayev's attitude towards his bikes?
12 What did Martin think was special about BMWs?
13 Why was Joe Catch offering his BSA so cheaply?
14 Why does Mr Manayev let Martin have the bike for £20 less than he had asked at first?

Judging the story

15 What impression do you get of Mr Manayev?
16 What do you think of the way Martin went about buying the bike from him?

Section D Writing

1 What have you learned from this story about the business of buying and selling second-hand motorbikes?
2 This story tells us quite a lot about Martin and Jake and how they get on together. Write a story about what happens to them in some other situation. Choose your own title, or write about one of these:

    The robbery
    The accident
    The big race

2 FORTUNE TELLING

Section A Omens

Ten words have been missed out in this section. They are listed at the end of the passage together with ten words that do not belong in the extract.

☐ Read the passage and decide which word should go in each space.

☐ Write the number of each space and against it write the word you have chosen.

There is hardly anything which moves which has not at one time served as an omen, hardly any human activity which was not surrounded with its own superstitions. The direction a bed faced has been thought — 1 —: for riches, the head should be to the East, for a long life, to the South. Money was supposed to come to you if you sneezed to the right, good news if you dropped and smashed an egg or had a shoelace which kept coming — 2 —.

Fortune might attend you if you picked up a pin, met the same person twice on the same journey or broke uncoloured glass (but if that glass was a — 3 — or a bottle then bad luck would follow). The sight of bellows and the burning of bones was once considered unlucky. If you wanted to avoid evil fortune you had, — 4 —, to not cut your hair before the new moon, avoid meeting grave-diggers, be careful never to cross two forks or two knives, and not mend clothes while you were — 5 — them. You should also never – unless you wanted to tempt fate – put your left shoe on before your right, break a pair of scissors, sit on a table without keeping one foot on the ground and, of course, never open an umbrella indoors.

It is as though everyone felt they were on the — 6 — of disaster all the time, kept from ill-fortune only by a series of inconsequential yet desperately important actions. At any moment one might unknow-ingly trigger off disaster. The spilling of salt, the breaking of a plate, even a sneeze – especially, it seems, on a Monday or Friday – could summon bad luck which had been lying in wait. If one believed all this then every action, every occurrence became an oracular pro-nouncement. All that was necessary was to know the appropriate meaning and one was then forewarned and prepared for what the future held in — 7 —.

People believed that Fate was constantly active and, therefore, that everything which occurred had a fateful message to convey. Every passing cloud, bird or breeze, every accident of nature, became part of the — 8 — by which one's future fate could be revealed so men scanned the earth and sky for omens.

Even now sometimes you probably catch yourself out not walking under a ladder, feeling slightly worried about breaking a mirror or waiting for the second magpie to — 9 —. It is not necessarily that you believe in such omens, just that having heard them from childhood there is a vague feeling that perhaps you might, after all, be tempting fate. And people who do disregard them – walking deliberately under every ladder they see – often do so with a certain air of defiance!

However, whether or not you choose to believe in them, certain — 10 — and phenomena have, over the centuries, been given particular meanings.

apparently apart so list code verge˙ significant˙ interesting˙ wearing˙ bite mirror˙ mending people undone˙ appear´ prison store rules events final

---

Section B Numerology

☐ Read the passage and then follow the instructions at the end.

Numbers stand for order. With mathematics a complex problem can be reduced to numerical terms and arrive at a logical conclusion. Because of this, because numbers can bring order out of apparent chaos, people have always attempted to manipulate numbers and use their power to unravel the complexities of human personality and life. Numbers therefore appear in many different ways and in several methods of fortune-telling.

The numbers are each linked to a planet, and it is the planet which suggests the major characteristics associated with the number.

One
The Sun Ambition, action, even aggression; but also creativity, individuality and the positive elements in character.

Two
The Moon Imagination, receptivity, artistic qualities; also balance and harmony.

Three
Jupiter Authority, conscientiousness, a strong sense of duty. Because this number also stands for the trinity it shows attachment to the family.

Four
Uranus Opposition, rebellion, reform. These traits are often coupled with idealism and a lack of worldly success.

Five
Mercury Excitable, highly strung, always searching for new adventures.

Six
Venus Attractive, even magnetic, with a love of beauty; easy to make friends with, trusting and to be trusted.

Seven
Neptune Love of travel. This is also the magic number so it stands for psychic powers.

Eight
Saturn Intensity and loneliness, extremism. This often indicates great success but at some cost to private happiness.

Nine
Mars Determination, will, aggression, a hastiness of temper, both courage and impulsiveness. This is the most important of the single numbers and is thought of as having great power.

Date of birth

In numerology, as in astrology, the subject's date of birth is important. This is to be expected as it is a personal set of numbers relating to the day on which he or she was born.

This date is simply converted to a Primary number. Just write the whole birth date out in figures, add them together once, then add together the result, until you are left with only a single figure. So, if the client was born on April 14th, 1945, the date in figures is 4.14.1945, which you write as the sum, 4+1+4+1+9+4+5. The answer, 28 gives you the sum 2+8, which in turn gives you the answer 10. And that, added together, gives the single number you need for the reading – the number 1.

Names

To give a deeper character analysis apply the divinatory power of numbers to the client's name and surname.

Numerical equivalents
This simple key gives a numerical equivalent for each letter.

A	B	C	D	E	F	G	H	I
J	K	L	M	N	O	P	Q	R
S	T	U	V	W	X	Y	Z	
1	2	3	4	5	6	7	8	9

Using this method the name 'Janet', for example, becomes 11552. Proceeding in the usual way this becomes the sum, 1+1+5+5+2 = 14. These two figures added together give you the Primary number 5.

Follow exactly the same method to reduce a surname to a Primary number.

☐ Work out the correct fortune for each of the people listed below. In each case, describe the fortune *using your own words*.

1 Yourself, using your own birthdate.
2 Someone born on 23rd May 1972.
3 Someone called Hugh Mason.
4 Someone called Fiona Blackadder.
5 Yourself, using your own name.

Section C   The dice

☐ Read the passage and then follow the instructions after it.

These deceptively simple little cubes with numbers marked upon them have been held to be responsible for making and breaking men's fortunes. The random nature of Fate is believed to be nowhere more clearly expressed than in the throwing of dice. Every throw is apparently completely unpredictable. The Egyptians knew these ancient toys, so did the Greeks. And throughout Asia precious woods and metals were used to make them in order to add to their latent power.

Method of reading

Dice have been used for divination for thousands of years, and methods of reading them have passed through many variations. There are, however, two absolute rules. For divination there must be three numbered dice, and they must be thrown in complete silence. It is also generally believed that they run more freely when the weather is calm and the atmosphere cool.

The most common method is to draw a simple chalk circle on a table and then throw the dice on behalf of the person whose fortune you are telling. Dice that roll beyond the circle have nothing to say. Those that fall on the floor indicate that disturbed and vexing times are ahead, which will probably be darkened by quarrels. If all the dice roll out of the circle, they should be picked up and thrown again. However, should the second throw also yield no result, it might be as well to assume that Fate has nothing to communicate that day, and wait until a more propitious moment.

There are two general points to remember. If a number turns up more than once during a reading, it presages the arrival of significant news. And on the very rare occasions when one dice lands on top of another it is always a warning that extreme caution should be exercised in all commercial and romantic ventures.

Meaning of numbers

Once the three dice have been rolled, add together the numbers shown on them. If one has rolled outside the circle and the total is less than three, the dice have nothing to say. The list which follows gives the most familiar meanings of the total numbers.

Three A good omen. A wish may be unexpectedly fulfilled.
Four Disappointment.
Five A stranger will bring joy.
Six Material loss from which some spiritual advantage may be gained.

Seven Unfounded gossip will cause unhappiness.

Eight A contemplated action has not been thought through, and may produce an injustice.

Nine Success, particularly in amorous affairs. If there has been a quarrel, expect reunion, forgiveness, reconciliation.

Ten Domestic contentment, and perhaps some professional or business advancement.

Eleven Someone – not necessarily a member of the family or close friend – is ill.

Twelve A letter will come, and an answer be demanded. Ask advice before coming to a decision.

Thirteen Grief, probably protracted, perhaps even lifelong.

Fourteen A stranger will become a close and dear friend.

Fifteen Temptation to enter into a shady or unjust deal.

Sixteen A journey. Take it, for it will pass pleasantly and end in profit.

Seventeen A man from overseas, probably a foreigner, will suggest a course of action to you. His suggestion will be sound.

Eighteen A very good omen – promotion, profit and joy.

1 For each of the following statements, say whether it is
       True
       False
       Impossible to tell from the passage
  a) There are many different ways of using dice to tell fortunes, but you must always use three dice.
  b) It does not make any difference if people talk while using the dice.
  c) You must always begin by drawing a circle.
  d) Quite often one dice lands on top of another.
  e) Asians used to think that dice made of materials like silver were better for fortune telling.

2 Explain in your own words what it means in each of the following cases:
  a) One dice has rolled off the table and the other two dice show one dot each.
  b) One dice lands on top of another.
  c) A dice falls on the floor.
  d) All three dice roll out of the circle – twice running.

3 Write down the correct fortune for each of the following throws. Use your own words.

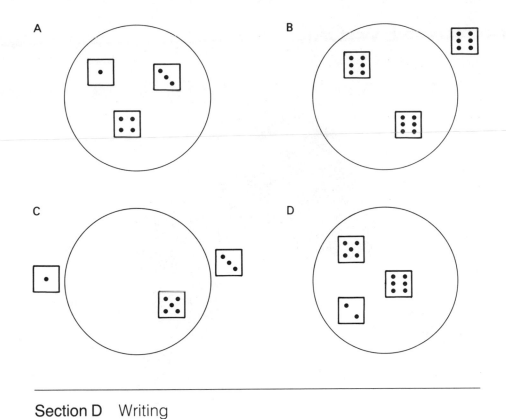

A   B   C   D

Section D   Writing

Using the information given in this unit, and/or any other knowledge you may have, write a story entitled *A Visit to the Fortune Teller*.

3 THE NEW CAR

Section A   Birthday present

In this section ten words have been missed out.

☐ Read the passage and work out a suitable word to fill each blank.

☐ Write the number of each blank and against it write the word you have chosen.

It was five days after my — 1 —. I was seventeen and five days. Tuesday, November 25th. Raining. I took the bus because it was raining so — 2 — when I got out of school. There was only one seat left. I sat down and tried to get the back of my neck away from my collar, which had got wet while I waited at the bus stop and felt like the Icy Hand of Death. And I sat there and felt — 3 —. About taking the bus.

Guilty about taking the bus. About taking the *bus*. Listen, the really — 4 — thing about being young is the triviality.

The reason I felt guilty about taking the bus is this. It was five days since my birthday, — 5 —? For my birthday my father had given me a present. A really fantastic present. It was — 6 —. He must have planned it and — 7 — for it for years, literally. He had it there waiting when I got home from school. It was parked in front of the house but I didn't even — 8 — it. He kept hinting, but I didn't get the hints. Finally he had to take me out and show it to me. When he gave me the keys his face got all — 9 — up as if he felt like crying with pride and pleasure.

It was a car, of course. I won't say the brand name because I think there's enough advertising around already. It was a new car. Clock, radio, all the — 10 —. It took him an hour to show me all the extras.

Section B The problem

This section has been divided into eight parts. Except for the first, they have been printed in the wrong order.

☐ Read them through, and work out the order they should be in.

☐ Write the numbers in that order.

I had learned to drive, and got my licence in October. It seemed useful, if there was an emergency, and I could do some errands for my mother, and get off by myself that way.

1 For that kind of money I could have lived for a year or more at the Massachusetts Institute of Technology, if I got a tuition scholarship. That's what came into my head right away, before he'd even opened the shiny little door. He could have put the money into savings. Of course, I could sell the car, and not take too bad a loss on it if I did it soon.

2 I didn't ask, but it was at least three thousand dollars. My father is a Chartered Accountant and we don't have that kind of money for unnecessary things.

3 The trouble came when he found out on Monday that I hadn't driven my new car to school. Why not?

4 She had a car, my father had a car, now I had a car. Three people, three cars. Only the thing was, I didn't want a car.
   What did the thing cost?

5   That came into my head too, and that was when he put the keys in my hand and said, 'She's all yours, son!' and his face twisted up that way.
    And I smiled. I guess.

6   That sounds as if I was scornful of him. I don't mean it that way.
    We took the car out for a ride right away, of course. I drove up into the Park, and he drove it back – he was itching to get his hands on the wheel – and all that was fine.

7   I don't know if I fooled him. If so, it was probably the first time I had ever succeeded in fooling anybody; but I think so, because he wanted so badly to be fooled, to believe that I was struck dumb with joy and gratitude.

Section C   My reasons

☐ Read the passage through and follow the instructions at the end.

a)   I couldn't tell him why not.
b)   I only half understood it myself.
c)   If I drove the thing to school and parked it in the school car park, I'd given in.
d)   I owned it.
e)   It owned me.
f)   I was the owner of a new car with all the extras.
g)   People at school would say, 'Hey, how about that. Hey wow. How about Fastback Griffiths!'
h)   Some of them would sneer, but some of them would honestly admire it, and maybe me for being lucky enough to own it.
i)   And that's what I couldn't take.
j)   I didn't know who I was, but I knew one thing: I wasn't the seat-fixture of an automobile.
k)   What I was was the type who walks to school (it's 2.7 miles by the shortest route) because walking is the kind of exercise I like, and I really like the streets of the city.
l)   The pavements, the buildings, the people you pass.
m)   Not the brake lights on the back of the car in front of you.
n)   Well, anyhow, that was where I drew the line.
o)   I'd already tried very ingeniously to hide the line, by driving errands for Mother on Saturday, and volunteering to take both

my parents for a drive in the country on Sunday in 'my new car'.
p) But Monday evening he found the line.
q) Didn't you take the car to school?
r) . Why not?
s) So there I was on Tuesday on the bus feeling guilty.
t) I wasn't even walking, after all my explanations of how I liked to walk and doctors say the exercise of walking is the best of all for the human body.
u) I was on the bus.
v) For twenty-five cents.
w) And three thousand dollars' worth of car was sitting on its white sidewall steel-belted radials in front of our house, right where I'd get off the bus.

☐ In this section the storyteller tries to sort out his own thoughts and feelings about the car.

1 The car is an *expensive possession*. Some of the sentences explain his feelings about possessions and the ways they affect other people. Write the numbers of these sentences.
2 Some of the sentences explain his feelings about *travelling through the city*. Write the numbers of these.
3 Some sentences explain how he tried to hide his feelings and trick his parents. Write the numbers of these.

☐ Now you can use the research you have done to help you answer these questions. Use your own words.

4 How did the storyteller think that people's opinions of him might change if they discovered he had a new car?
5 Why did he prefer to walk to school?
6 How did he try to trick his parents?
7 Explain in your own words what you think he means by 'the line' in sentences 14, 15, and 16.

___

Section D   Writing

'. . . Monday evening he found the line . . .' Write the conversation you imagine took place between the boy and his father on that Monday evening.

4 THE PROFESSOR

Section A An interesting smell

This unit is taken from a longer story. This means that it may be more difficult to work out what is going on. Imagine that you have the author by you as you read the extract: what questions would you like to be able to ask him about it?

☐ As you reach each asterisk (*), stop reading.

☐ Write down at least one question that you would like to ask him.

☐ Then continue to the next asterisk.

     Smiler woke the next morning just as the sun was coming up. The rain had gone. Early morning traffic was beginning to move up and down the road. Stiffly, he and Bacon emerged from their pipe and went back over the hedge to get away from the road.* Both of them
5 were damp, bedraggled and hungry. They ploughed through the wet

long grass of a meadow, the grass starred with tall ox-daisies and
creamy spikes of meadow-sweet above which the bees were already
long busy. The top of the meadow was bounded by a small, fast-
running stream. Smiler took a look at the sun and saw that the stream
10 was running from the north to the south, so he began to move
upstream with Bacon at his heels.*

    After about a hundred yards Smiler suddenly stopped and raised
his head and sniffed. He sniffed two or three times and slowly his
mouth began to water. He looked down at Bacon and said, 'Bacon,
15 my lad – if there's one morning smell that you can't mistake it's eggs
and bacon frying.'*

    Slowly the two moved cautiously upstream, following the de-
licious smell. They came to a small clump of willows growing at the
stream side and went into them. The smell grew stronger. In the
20 middle of the clump, close to the stream's edge, they saw a large sheet
of black plastic material which had been tied in a canopy between four
trees with the loose ends pegged down on three sides to make a snug
shelter. The opening faced away from them. Over the top of the
sheeting a thin, blue curl of wood smoke showed and the smell of
25 cooking was very pungent and appetizing.*

    With Bacon close to his heels Smiler moved around the side of the
shelter. Just in front of it was a small fire, burning in a neat fireplace
made from stones taken from the stream. On the fire was a large
frying-pan which held four rashers of bacon, two eggs and a sausage,
30 all sizzling gently away. It was a sight which made Smiler's midriff
ache. Sitting just outside the tent affair on a small canvas folding stool
was a man with a long twig in his hand with which he was turning the
sausage and bacon as they cooked.*

    He looked up at Smiler without surprise.* Then he looked at
35 Bacon. And then he looked back at Smiler and slowly winked.

    Smiler, anxious to establish good relations, said politely, 'Good
morning, sir.'

1 Look at the questions you have written.
   a) Are there any of them that you can now answer?
   b) Put a tick against any that you can answer.
2 Study the remaining questions and work out the best answer you
   can to each one.
3 Discuss your questions and answers with a partner.

☐ Read the passage and follow the instructions at the end.

The man said, 'Good morning, boy.' He looked Smiler up and
down again and it was the kind of look that missed nothing. Then he
said, 'A good morning after a bad night. How did you and your
companion, *canis mongrelis*, make out?'

'Not very well, sir,' said Smiler. 'We slept in a drainpipe by the
road back there.'

The man nodded. 'In my time I have done the same, but it is not to
be recommended. Man was not framed to sleep on the arc of a circle.
It is a question of the relative inflexibility of the human spine. I
presume that it was the aroma of a traditional English breakfast that
brought you this way?'

'We're both pretty hungry, sir. That's if you've got enough to
spare. I could pay for it. I've got some money and –'

The man raised a warning hand. 'Please, boy – do not mention
money. Friendship and shared adversity are the only coinage recog-
nized by true gentlemen of the road. Would I be right in putting you
at two eggs and three rashers – plus a sausage? And for your faithful
hound I have an old ham bone somewhere in my gear and he can
have the pleasure of licking the frying-pan clean later.'

'Gosh!' said Smiler. 'That would be jolly super – if you can spare
it.'

'Say no more.'

The man turned, reached back into his shelter, and dragged out a
battered old perambulator with a tatty folded hood and began to
ferret in it for provisions. In no time at all he had found eggs, bacon
and sausage and they were in the frying-pan. The ham bone was
unwrapped from an old newspaper and handed to Bacon. Then from
the battered pram the man pulled out another folding canvas stool
and handed it to Smiler saying, 'Rest your juvenile posterior on that.'

Smiler opened up the stool, sat down, and watched the man as he
now began to give serious application to the cooking of an extra
breakfast.

He was a funny-looking old boy, thought Smiler. He had long
black hair to his shoulders and a straggling black beard. His face was
brown and furrowed with wrinkles. Above a nobly beaked nose his
eyes were as bright as a hedge-sparrow's eggs. Smiler, who wasn't
much good at guessing ages, felt he must be much older than his
father. For clothes, starting at the top, he wore a bowler hat whose
blackness had a nice green shine like verdigris on copper, and his
jacket was made of green and brown tweed and was patched and

torn. His trousers were of blue denim and tucked into a pair of green gum boots. Underneath his open jacket he wore a red T-shirt on the front of which was a printed head of a man with long flowing hair and the word – Beethoven – under it.

1 a) Make a list of any words in the passage that you do not understand. Leave two lines underneath each word before writing the next.
   b) Look at the sentence each word is in. Try to work out the meaning of each word from the way it is used. Alongside each word write the meaning you have worked out.
   c) Now look the words up in a dictionary. If the meaning you have written is clearly wrong, write the correct meaning underneath.
2 The writer tells us quite a lot about the tramp's *appearance*.
   a) Make a list of all the details he gives us.
   b) Write a factual description of him, using the information in your list.
3 The writer also tells us about the man's character: what he is like as a person. Describe what you think he is like, based on your reading of this section.

Section C Professor

In this section seven sentences have been missed out. They are listed in the wrong order at the end.

☐ Read the passage and work out which sentence should go in each blank.

☐ Write the number of each blank and beside it write the letter of the sentence you have chosen.

The man looked up from his cooking and asked, 'And what would your name be, boy?'

For a moment Smiler hesitated. Then he decided that this man didn't look the kind who would read the newspapers much or listen to the radio, so he decided to tell the truth.

'————— 1 ————— Most people call me Smiler. But I don't care for it much.'

'Neither do I since I don't care for half-cooked puns any more than I do for half-cooked buns. I shall call you Samuel. And your four-legged friend?'

'That's Bacon.'

'A good name. Of course, after the great philosopher and not the comestible of that ilk.' Then seeing the baffled look on Smiler's face, he went on, 'Never mind. Allow me to introduce myself. —————— 2 ——————— That, of course, is my true name. I have others which necessity from time to time makes it desirable to employ. But then, as a gentleman of the road yourself, you, no doubt, understand that perfectly well.'

'Yes, of course, sir . . . I mean, Professor,' said Smiler.

'Capital, Samuel. We who live outside society must be allowed our little stratagems.'

'What are you a Professor of?' asked Smiler.

The Professor reached back into the pram for two plates and cutlery and said over his shoulder, 'I am a Professor of all the Ologies. You name one and I am a Professor of it.' ——————— 3 ——————— The sight and smell made Smiler's stomach feel hollow.

'Name an Ology,' said the Professor severely.

A bit stumped for the moment, all his eyes and attention on the coming breakfast, Smiler searched around in his mind desperately and finally said, '——————— 4 ———————'

A fine subject. One of the oldest. *Granite is hard and sandstone is soft, but Time's withering hand turns all to dust.* ——————— 5 ——————— Now let us eat while the water boils for our coffee.'

He handed Smiler his plate and knife and fork, put an old tin can full of water into the embers of the fire, and then began to attack his own breakfast.

The two of them tucked into their breakfast while, a little way to the side, Bacon cracked and gnawed at the last of his bone. A bluetit came and sat on a branch above the canopy, scolded them, and then flew down to investigate a slip of bacon rind that Smiler tossed into the bushes for it. The stream ran behind them, making a pleasant musical sound, and the morning sun slid higher and bathed them with its warmth. ——————— 6 ———————

Over his coffee, the Professor produced a small cheroot from the inside pocket of his jacket and lit it. He tipped his bowler hat back, blew a cloud of blue smoke, and contemplated Smiler. After a few moments he said, 'Well, Samuel, state your problem.'

A little guarded, Smiler said, 'Problem, Professor? What problem?'

The Professor shook his head. 'All mankind has problems. ——————— 7 ——————— Wandering about the country with a dog with a bit of string for a collar, carrying an old sack for luggage, spending a night in a concrete pipe – I don't have to be a Professor of Sociology to know you must have a problem.'

a) What about Geology?
b) And that includes boys.
c) He turned and began to dish the breakfast from the frying-pan with a knife and fork.
d) I am, you see, also a bit of a poet – although the rhyme is bad which is due to the early hour of the day.
e) Samuel Miles, Sir.
f) It was one of the best breakfasts Smiler could remember and it was crowned by the Professor's coffee which was strong and laced with liberal dollops of sweet condensed milk.
g) I am Professor Roscoe Bertram Crimples.

Section D   Writing

1   Think about these questions:
    a) Where has Smiler come from and why is he living rough?
    b) Will the Professor get the true story out of him?
    c) What will Smiler do next – stay with the Professor, or strike out on his own?
    d) What will the Professor do?
2   Now write your version of what happens next in the story.

5 KESTREL

Section A   The wood

In this section ten words have been replaced by other words that are not as suitable. These replacement words are printed in *italics*.

☐ Make a list of the words in italics.

☐ Think carefully about the sentences they are in and choose a more suitable word.

☐ Write your improvements beside the words in italics.

The moon was almost complete, its outline well *shown*, except for the blur on the waxing curve. The sky was cloudless, the air still warm, but when he reached the fields it cooled slightly, taking on a *new*, sharper quality. The moon made it light in the fields, and lent the grass a silver sheen, and the piebald hides of the cows were clearly visible in this silvery light. The wood was a narrow black band beyond the fields, *getting* taller and taller as Billy approached, until it formed a curtain stretched out before him, and the top of the curtain appeared to touch the stars *up* above.

He climbed on to the stile and looked into the trees. It was dark on both sides of the path, but above the path the foliage was thinner, and the light from the moon *came* and lit the way. Billy stepped down off the stile and entered the wood. The trunks and branches lining the path formed pillars and lintels, terraced doorways leading into dark interiors. He hurried by them, *seeing* in, right and left. A scuffle to his left. He side-stepped to the right and began to run, the *noise* of his feet and the rasp of his breath filtering far into the trees. WO-HU-WO-HOOOO. WO-HU-WO-HOOOO. He stopped and listened, trying to control his breathing. WO-HU-WO-HOOO. Somewhere ahead; the long falter radiating back through the trees. Billy *joined* his fingers, placed his thumbs together and blew into the split between them. The only sound he produced was that of rushing air. He licked his lips and tried again, producing a wheeze, which he swiftly worked up into a single hoot and developed into a strident imitation of the tawny owl's call. He listened. There was no *sound*, so he repeated it, this time working for the softer, more wavering sound, by stuttering his breath into the sound chamber. And out it came, as clear and as clean as a blowing of bubbles. His call was immediately answered. Billy grinned and answered back. He started to walk again, and *made* contact with the owl for the rest of the distance through the wood.

Section B   The nest

This section has been divided into ten parts. Except for the first, these have been printed in the wrong order.

☐ Work out the order they should be in.

☐ Write the numbers in that order.

The farmhouse was in darkness. Billy carefully climbed over the wall into the orchard and ran crouching across to the ruins. He stood back from the wall and looked up at it.

1   Occasionally he dislodged a small stone or a lump of plaster, and when he felt this happen he paused during the time of its fall, and for a time after it had landed.

But there were no alarms, and he reached the window and hooked his left arm over the stone sill.

31

2 By a process of elimination, he placed them back into the nest until he was left with only one; the one with most feathers and only a little down on its head. He lowered it back into the pocket, then held his hand up to catch the light of the moon. Both back and palm were bleeding and scratched, as though he had been nesting in a hawthorn hedge.

   When he reached the bottom of the wall he opened his jacket and clucked down into the pocket.

3 If any stones moved he felt again, remaining still until he was satisfied. Slowly. Hand. Foot. Hand. Foot. Never stretching, never jerking. Always compact, always balanced.

4 He felt around, then withdrew his hand grasping a struggling eyas kestrel. He sat up, caged the bird in his hands, then placed it carefully into the big pocket inside his jacket. Five times he felt into the hole and each time fetched out a young hawk.

5 He slapped the stone and sh sh'd at the hole at the other end of the sill. Nothing happened so he climbed astride and hutched across to the nest hole. He peered in, but there was nothing to see, so he stretched belly flop along the sill and felt into the hole, wriggling further along as his arm went further in.

6 The moon illuminated the face of the wall, picking out the jut of individual stones, and shading in the cracks and hollows between them. Billy selected his route, found a foothold, a handhold, and began to climb. Very slowly and very carefully, testing each hold thoroughly before trusting it with his weight. His fingers finding the spaces, then tugging at the surrounding stones as though testing loose teeth.

7 Sometimes crabbing to by-pass gaps in the stonework, sometimes back-tracking several moves to explore a new line; but steadily meandering upwards, making for the highest window.

   As he climbed, his feet and hands dislodged a trickle of plaster and stone dust, and birds brushed his knuckles as they flashed out of their nest holes.

8   The weight at the bottom stirred. He placed one hand underneath it for support, and set off back across the orchard. Once over the wall, he started to whistle, and he whistled and hummed to himself all the way home. . . .

9   Some were slightly larger than others, some more fully feathered, with less down on their backs and heads, but each one came out gasping, beaks open, legs pedalling the air.

    When he had emptied the nest he reversed the procedure, dipping into his pocket for an eyas and holding it in one hand while he compared it with another.

Section C   Training

Billy keeps his kestrel in a shed at home. Each day he trains it. In this section the author describes part of that training.

☐ Read the passage and answer the questions at the end.

He unlocked the shed door, slipped inside and closed it quietly behind him. The hawk was perched on a branch which had been wedged between the walls towards the back of the shed. The only other furniture in the shed were two shelves, one fixed behind the bars of the door, the other high up on the wall. The walls and ceiling were whitewashed, and the floor had been sprinkled with a thick layer of dry sand, sprinkled thicker beneath the perch and the shelves. The shelf on the door was marked with two dried mutes, both thick and white, with a central deposit of faeces as crozzled and black as the burnt ends of matches.

    Billy approached the hawk slowly, regarding it obliquely, clucking and chanting softly, 'Kes Kes Kes.' The hawk bobbed her head and shifted along the perch. Billy held out his gauntlet and offered her a scrap of beef. She reached forward and grasped it with her beak, and tried to pull it from his glove. Billy gripped the beef tightly between forefinger and thumb; and in order to obtain more leverage, the hawk stepped on to his fist. He allowed her to take the beef, then replaced her on the perch, touching the backs of her legs against the wood so that she stepped backwards on to it. He dipped into the leather satchel at his hip and offered her a fresh scrap; this time holding it just out of range of her reaching beak. She bobbed her head and tippled forward slightly, regained balance, then glanced about, uncertain, like someone up on the top board for the first time.

'Come on, Kes. Come on then.'

He stood still. The hawk looked at the meat, then jumped on to the glove and took it. Billy smiled and replaced it with a tough strip of beef, and as the hawk busied herself with it, he attached a swivel to the ends of the jesses dangling from her legs, slipped the jesses between the first and second fingers of his glove, and felt into his bag for the leash. The hawk looked up from her feeding. Billy rubbed his finger and thumb to make the meat move between them, and as the hawk attended to it again, he threaded the leash through the lower ring of the swivel and pulled it all the way through until the knot at the other end snagged on the ring. He completed the security by looping the leash twice round his glove and tying the end round his little finger.

He walked to the door and slowly pushed it open. The hawk looked up, and as he moved out into the full light, her eyes seemed to expand, her body contract as she flattened her feathers. She bobbed her head, once, twice, then bated, throwing herself sideways off his glove and hanging upside down, thrashing her wings and screaming. Billy waited for her to stop, then placed his hand gently under her breast and lifted her back on to the glove. She bated again; and again, and each time Billy lifted her carefully back up, until finally she stayed up, beak half open, panting, glaring round.

'What's up then? What's a matter with you, Kes? Anybody'd think you'd never been out before.'

The hawk roused her feathers and bent to her meat, her misdemeanours apparently forgotten.

1 Draw a diagram of the shed and show where each of these things was:

    shelves   branch   sand   hawk

2 The main things that Billy did are listed below, but they are in the wrong order. Write the letters in the order in which the things actually happened.

a) He offered it a second piece of meat.
b) He went slowly up to the hawk.
c) He fixed the leash to the jesses.
d) The hawk stepped onto his fist to eat it.
e) He took the hawk outside.
f) He entered the shed.
g) He tied the leash to his hand.
h) He offered it the first piece of meat and it ate it.
i) While it was eating he gripped the jesses between his fingers.

3   The passage uses a number of words you may not have seen before:

   mutes   gauntlet   jesses   leash   bate

Find them in the passage. Write each one down, allowing plenty of space. Work out your own definition of each one and write it down beside the word. If you don't know the word have a guess, based on how it is used.

When you have done *all* the words try looking them up in a dictionary. You may have to use more than one dictionary.

Section D   Writing

Billy was not a great success at school. His kestrel was the only thing he was really interested in. In an English lesson one day the teacher, Mr Farthing, got him to talk about it.

'Now then Billy, tell me about this hawk. Where did you get it from?'

How do you think the conversation went? Write your own version of it.

6 THE BROKEN KNEE

George Mitchell took part in the Yukon Gold Rush at the end of the nineteenth century. He travelled right across Canada, often in the company of Indians. On his way he had many adventures.

Section A The accident

In this section twelve words have been missed out.

☐ Read the passage through and try to work out what the missing words are.

☐ Write the number of each blank and against it write the word you have chosen.

Francis called a — 1 — on a bench just up from the river, and for some reason I set to work to cut down a spruce tree – a good-sized one it was, twelve inches or so on the stump. I'd cut almost right — 2 — it, and struck it higher up with the back of the axe to pitch it, when the damn tree butted the wrong way and the cursed butt hit me fair on the — 3 — of my left knee, which was forward. I sat down hard in the snow, and was surprised to see the — 4 — of my foot under my left elbow. My leg wouldn't straighten of itself, and the knee seemed to work both ways without any check. The pain, of course, was — 5 —.

Francis was simply wonderful. He lifted me gently up, laid me on a moose hide, and made me as comfortable as he could with — 6 — robes. Then he had a council with the Indians, which lasted for a long time with tremendous gesticulation and excitement. When this was over he told me very — 7 — and kindly that he would take me away to his own winter camp, sixty miles farther on up-stream and back from the river, where he had — 8 — the squaws to be out of range of passing miners.

The Indians got busy at once, and in an incredibly short time they had cut me a pair of splints that reached from the thigh to the — 9 —, and bound them on very firmly with moose-hide thongs – dog-traces I guess they were. Then they fitted side-pieces and a back to one of the toboggans to make a cariole of it, — 10 — it well with furs for me to lie on, and lifted me and my leg in and tied me securely so that I shouldn't fall out going over — 11 — ground. Francis himself covered me up most carefully with furs, and put a big moose skin on top of it all – and I — 12 — all that and a sight more as it must have been a good forty-five or fifty below.

Section B   The journey

This section has been divided into seven parts. The first part has been printed at the beginning, but the remaining six parts have been jumbled up.

☐ Read them through and work out what the correct order should be. Write the numbers in that order.

Then Francis harnessed up the six best dogs, took two more on leashes for spares, and started with his best runner for what I think was one of the quickest dashes Indians had ever made.

1   But this was very happily done by Flora, who loved cutting – the more she hurt the patient the better she liked it!

2   The squaws rapidly cleared a sleeping-space for me, tossed up the boughs and laid out clean fur rugs, and I was carefully lifted out of the toboggan and deposited.

Now I didn't know at all what the Indians had in mind to do about my leg, but I thought that even if I came through alive I should probably not be in shape to do anything after they'd finished with me. So, in spite of great pain, I got them to set me with my head and shoulders up, and before I let them start work I wrote a note to Jack at Wind City and another to Cecil at the Pass.

3   We did the sixty-odd miles in just about eleven hours. First we dropped down into the river-bed and then went up-river for miles and miles, sometimes on the hummocky ice and sometimes taking a short cut over the banks – the toboggan bumping and crashing and sometimes swinging round sideways like a pendulum when we crossed a bit of sloping ground. If I'd been compos I'd have been afraid of getting brained alive; but as it was I think I passed out pretty often though it seemed like eternity just the same.

4   These notes were short and to the point – 'Follow this Indian and come quick. Broke leg.' Francis sent them off at once, each with two good men, and then I said to carry on and do their damnedest.

Now you must understand, Graham, that surgery, among my Indians, was entirely an affair for the women. Old Colin's wife Jane, and the young girl Flora, Francis' wife, were both surgeons – old Jane had learned the Indian medicine and surgery from childhood, but strange to say, though she would examine any case and give her diagnosis, the actual cutting she never would do, being much too kind-hearted.

5   Francis headed straight for his own lodge, which was in the middle of the camp, and after he had given his people instructions to clear a space in the lodge the moose hide that formed the door was taken down and the toboggan was picked up and carried inside.

6   At last we turned off into a side-valley and climbed up the benches, and I remember coming back to consciousness as we topped a rise and getting my first view of the Indians' winter lodges.

We drove down the slope to the lodges at a break-neck pace, with the men yelling like fury, and all the Indians turned out to meet us in great excitement.

☐ Read the passage through and then answer the questions that follow it.

First they removed the rough splints that Francis' men had made and old Jane gave instructions to two expert woodworkers to smooth them down and make them take practically the shape of the leg – one from the ankle to the groin and the other from the ankle to the thigh. (They worked this with their crooked knives, which are A1 for that sort of carving and whittling when you know how to use them.) Then she ripped up my breeches – I had on two pairs of light caribou with clipped fur – and laid bare the leg, which was black, green, and purple, and so swollen that even the toes were standing out independently. Both women examined it very carefully and after quite a short parley decided what they ought to do.

They began by putting on the splints, before they did any cutting, with a covering of duffle and old blanketing above and below the knee that left the region of the knee itself well exposed. Then they broke some flint flakes with sharp cutting edges off a block of flint that they kept for striking lights, and Flora started her business. I asked Francis later why they used flint flakes instead of an ordinary knife, and he said that a fresh flint flake was clean while a steel knife-blade would have been dirty.

Flora made her first cut, about three inches long, inside the knee and upwards: this didn't bleed freely and what blood there was came out clotted, but it gave a feeling of relief and I urged them to press the blood out. Then she made another cut cross-ways below the knee and a third like the first, up the outer side of the leg, and after these cuts the blood came much more freely. Then she seized the U-shaped flap of skin and flesh that she had just released on the two sides and bottom and flayed it up and back, exposing the knee-cap; it was split right across from side to side with the two halves drawing away from one another upwards and downwards.

Old Jane had evidently known what she was going to find and had set some men to make a lot of little pins out of caribou bone. Now she forced the two halves of the knee-cap together and the other little bird drove in the pins below the base of the lower half and above the top of the upper half, and then wound them very firmly together, figure-of-eight, with the fine strong sinews taken from the back of a caribou and pulled out to about the thickness of the coarsest sewing-thread. Then they put back the flap of skin and bound it into place with thongs, without any stitching.

39

I don't know how long all this pleasant process took; it may have been two or three hours – anyhow, it was dark all the time except for the firelight. I tried to carry off the first part of the game with a high head – had my cutty pipe and tried to pretend there was nothing wrong. But I must have passed out more than once, as I would waken up to find little bags of moose skin with hot ashes in them in the palms of my hands, which they used to revive me when they thought I had been out too long and perhaps might not come back otherwise.

. . . . .

When Mitchell returned to civilization the doctors found his knee-cap perfectly knit. His leg was naturally stiff, as he had worn his splints continuously, and a long spell of treatment was required to restore the withered muscles and to loosen the stiff joint. But the leg was eventually brought back to a perfectly sound condition – so much so that he was able to break it again thirty-three years later in a different place, having also broken his right leg, for good measure, in the interim.

1   What did the Indians do to the splints?
2   Why were Mitchell's toes 'standing out independently'?
3   What 'knives' did the women use and why?
4   How did they join the two parts of the knee cap together?
5   How did Mitchell behave while the operation was going on?
6   How did the Indians revive him when he passed out?
7   Was the operation a success?

Section D   Writing

Think about
a)   *how* the Indians treated Mitchell, a white man;
b)   *what* they were able to do for him.
Write two paragraphs expressing the conclusions you have reached.

7 PROFESSIONAL SINGER

Section A Learning to sing

☐ Read the passage and follow the instructions at the end.

Terri Balash is a lively, gregarious twenty-four year old who says of
performing, 'it's in my blood'. She always wanted to perform. At six
she urged her mother to put her into the modelling business (in those
days she had golden curls and looked like Shirley Temple) and even
5 earlier she used to march precociously into her parents' parties and
announce 'Okay, I'm going to entertain now, so everybody listen'.

At five she began dancing lessons, at six she started learning the
recorder, at eight the violin, and as her grandmother was a piano
teacher she picked up that instrument young too. Did she ask for all
10 these lessons, or was she pushed into them by her parents? 'I don't
remember,' she answers, 'I was a child of culture; birthday presents
were the ballet with grandma.' It's all so much a part of her now that
how it all began does not really seem to matter.

Singing has always been there, but she did not take singing
15 lessons until three years ago. 'I didn't take them when I was young
because it's not a good idea. Just like boys', girls' voices go through a

change when they grow up. But more than that, there was this fear of handing my voice over to someone else to do something with. There are good voice teachers and bad voice teachers, and a bad one can do
20 irreparable damage. It's kind of scary.' In fact, in her teens she took a couple of private lessons one year when she was acting in an amateur production of *As You Like It* and vividly remembers the effect: 'I remember coming out after a half hour of vocalization so tight and in such pain that I knew there must be something wrong. Singing
25 wrong will produce nodes, little nodules on your vocal chords, which sometimes can be surgically removed. But singers who sing correctly can sing for hours and hours and really never feel it. It's a muscle, the more you use it the stronger and healthier it is. But if you sing wrongly you can do a lot of damage. So I lived with that kind of fear
30 for a long time.'

When Terri eventually took voice lessons she was astonished by the results and now believes that with the *right* teacher they are vital for a young singer. 'Singing is a very easy natural thing for me and I thought maybe he'd try to change something and I wouldn't sound
35 like me anymore. I found instead that he didn't change my voice. It still sounded like me, just better. He freed my whole voice and today I still feel the effects. I couldn't tell you what he did, but it changed my ability to sing for long periods and to get placement.' Now she feels she needs to get back into training. Opera singers study all their lives,
40 and though she doesn't aspire to be an opera singer she realizes the great value of a trained voice.

'It's a cliché,' says Terri, 'but you sing from your diaphragm. You must breathe correctly and that requires muscle control and muscle tone and being in shape. When you see rock singers running around
45 on stage and singing out of breath they're singing on their vocal chords. Take Janis Joplin – a classic example of a wrecked voice. She could hardly talk.'

One of the drawbacks to private lessons, however, is the cost. It's essential to go to somebody good, and the good teachers are expen-
50 sive, starting at about $20 an hour. How often you go depends on how successful you are at practising on your own. If you can vocalize correctly at home then an hour a week may be enough. If you can't, it isn't. Ideally, Terri says she would like to take two or three lessons a week but there is the permanent lack of money.

Research

Two main topics are discussed in this section:
  Terri Balash's early life
  Voice lessons

1 Which sentences are mainly concerned with her early life?
   Write the numbers of the lines in which these sentences begin.

Example:

> performing, 'it's in my blood'. She always wanted to perform. At six
> she urged her mother to put her into the modelling business (in those
> days she had golden curls and looked like Shirley Temple) and even
> 5 earlier she used to march precociously into her parents' parties and
> announce 'Okay, I'm going to entertain now, so everybody listen'.
>   At five she began dancing lessons, at six she started learning the

You write: line 2
          line 7

2 Do the same for the sentences about voice lessons.
3 Some of the sentences about voice lessons explain their advantages, while some are about their disadvantages. Make two separate lists of the numbers you wrote for question 2, one showing the advantages and the other the disadvantages.

Writing

4 Using your own words, write a short factual account of Terri's early life.
5 Write two paragraphs in your own words: one explaining the advantages of voice lessons, the other explaining their disadvantages.

Section B Starting a career

This section is divided into nine parts. Except for the first, these have been printed in the wrong order.

☐ Read them through and work out the correct order.

☐ Write the numbers in that order.

Singing well is not just a matter of voice training. You have to be in good shape to give a performance everything. It is exhausting work and stamina is essential.

1 To date she has appeared in five productions of the musical and, though she swore she would never do it again, she is about to direct a sixth herself, in Toronto. Constant work like that, however, is not always as idyllic as it might seem.

2   Recently she has been trying to break into the club circuit, but finds it both difficult and expensive for a young performer.

Last year she got a break when a friend suggested her as a substitute for the Boltax Club in New York where an act had been cancelled at the last minute. Terri had no act, no material, no agent, no pianist and ten days to organize the performance. Success, however, is partly talent, partly luck, but largely making the most of opportunities. Fortunately her room-mate, Carolyn, is a theatrical producer and had the time and ability to step into the role of temporary manager, so much so that she even managed to extract a small singing fee from the club.

3   Terri believes her dancing lessons have been invaluable, likewise her acting experience: 'There are singers and there are well-rounded performers. I aspire to be a well-rounded performer, not just sing songs. I think a singer is someone who can really put a song across. A singer is an actress. Like Bette Midler. Her ballads are drop-dead unbelievable.'

Starting out on her career as a singer Terri had the luck to get a part singing in *Godspell* with some of the cast from the New York company.

4   She has, after all, been working with theatres since her first job at the age of seventeen when she did *Jacques Brel* in her hometown in New Jersey for $10 a night. 'I'm in a transitional phase,' she says. 'I'm rehearsing with a rock group a little, but I'm finding that my heart lies in getting on the stage and being Terri the singer.'

5   Musicians must be paid for rehearsal as well as performance time, invitations must be sent out, mailing shots paid for, and then the young singer has to buy something special to wear. Expenses for the show came to about $600, and even then Terri got away relatively cheaply because the act only involved herself and a piano, and the pianist did not have to write any charts for the accompaniment (usually an added expense that can cost $1000 if several instruments are involved). Since the Boltax, Terri has appeared at the Fives Club, also in New York, but still owes Carolyn $300 from the Boltax appearance.

6   This is rare for a young performer as so many singers are looking for showcases for their talent in New York and most will appear willingly without pay just for the chance of being heard. Terri and Carolyn put

the act together in nine days but found it very expensive. 'It's exorbitant when you have to pay to get somebody to play for you,' explains Terri.

7   It meant she learned the original choreography and direction. The result has been a steady source of work, as she explains, 'Godspell is like a skill. If you have to put a Godspell company together fast, you want someone who knows it because it's a hard show – it's ten people on stage all of the time.'

8   It can mean no movies, no plays, no dinner-parties, no holidays and at times continuous touring during which the glamour can wear a bit thin. 'The bottom line is when you're out in Oshkosh, travelling around in a bus.'
    Terri gravitates more towards club singing than musical theatre now. 'Godspell is about energy and innocence and you get to be an old, tired Godspell clown and it just doesn't work. It's a way to make a living, and it's safe, but I don't want to be safe.' Directing, she feels, is different, but she doesn't want to stay in musical theatre permanently.

Section C   The way ahead

☐   The whole article about Terri Balash is based on an interview. As you read this section work out what questions she must have been asked. Make a list of the questions.

Financing your own act is not the only way to break into the club circuit. An alternative would be to try to perform enough in Broadway, or anywhere you can make a reputation, and hope to attract audiences to club dates. From the Boltax to the Fives Club, for example, Terri found she had doubled the audience, and says with pleasure 'People would come up and say "would you put us on your mailing list, because we want to be there next time." It blows my mind.'
    Her plans for the future include auditioning for a Broadway show, or getting a band together or trying to get into recording or commercials. Of her career she says, 'It's a business, it's a job', but is determined that she'll enjoy it. 'I can't justify going to nine to five jobs just because you feel you have to. It's your life and you'd better enjoy

it while you're here. It's too easy to wake up ten, twenty, thirty years later and say – where did the time go, I was doing something I hated.' Not that Terri has any illusions about the realities of the business, as she says: 'I love recording and that's where I hope I'm headed. But if you're gonna cut an album or go on the road six or eight months or whatever, that's it, you know what you give up – you give up your life. You don't get to hang around your apartment in your blue jeans anymore.' The difficult decisions, however, are the professional ones.

Whether to invest two to five years, or however many years it takes to get to a Broadway show so that she can do what she wants to afterwards. Whether to concentrate on advertising work, which is less arduous but means dropping something else. 'Commercial work is fun, it's relatively easy and it's great bucks, but it means spending your energies and I would have to put other things on hold.' She knows for certain, though, that she cannot do all these things: 'I need to focus my energy. If I'm going to go for a Broadway show, I need to go to every audition. I can't diffuse now. I need to focus in on something, to try and get in touch with what I want.'

Her cabaret singing spot has opened a whole new world to her, and she thinks it's the way she would like to develop. 'I'm just starting to find out that I think my vocal tendency is going to easy-going middle of the road rock. My voice is even changing; it's getting into a more contemporary sound.' In her shows at the Boltax and the Fives Clubs she sang some soul, some light rock, like Melissa Manchester and some musical numbers such as a song from *Company* by Stephen Sondheim. 'My dream,' she says, 'is to sing in front of a big sound. I love that big band sound, that old Tommy Dorsey stuff.

Something happens to me when I get on stage. Something takes over. I am different than when I am sitting here just talking, but it's still me. You know when you're on stage and there's the footlights between you and the audience, you can't get enough applause and it's the most wonderful thing.'

Section D   Writing

---

1   What impression have you formed of Terri Balash?
    Write a paragraph describing what you think she is like as a person.
2   Imagine that you had the opportunity to interview her for the school magazine. Make a list of ten questions you would like to ask her.

8 ACCIDENT

This unit consists of the first three pages of a novel, *Empty World* by
John Christopher. At the beginning of a novel the author has to set
the scene: tell the reader who the characters are, where the story takes
place and so on. Sometimes this is done in a straightforward way, but
at other times it is not so simple. In *Empty World* John Christopher
makes us work to puzzle out what is going on.

Section A The dream

□ Read the passage through *once* and then answer the questions without looking back.

*They were driving along the motorway on a bright sunny morning, everyone
happy. While Neil's father drove, his mother was telling him something about
a dance at the golf club. Amanda and Andy were arguing, but amiably, about
a pop programme they had watched on TV. Grandpa and Grandma were
admiring the countryside, he pointing out a view that attracted him and she*

agreeing. Neil himself was silent, engrossed in a strange but satisfying feeling
of well-being. He tried to work out what had given rise to it, but could not. It
being end of term, the try he had scored in the junior House final, the prospect
of summer and the cricket season ahead? Or perhaps just this journey.

He could not decide, but it did not matter. He was relaxing in the
enjoyment of that, too – it not mattering – when he heard his mother's small
gasping cry and looked up to see it: the monstrous hulk of the heavy lorry and
trailer jack-knifing across the road in front of them, looming up and up. . . .
Then screams, and blackness, and he woke up sweating, his fingers digging
into the bed clothes that were wrapped tightly round him.

Neil thought about the dream later that day, as he walked across
the churchyard on his way to catch the bus to school. It had been full
of inaccuracies and impossibilities, the way dreams were. Not a
sunny morning, but a dull rain-bleared afternoon. Not a motorway,
but the A21, a few miles south of the Tonbridge bypass. And, of
course, Grandpa and Grandma had not been there. The Rover was a
roomy car, but not that roomy; and besides, the object of the journey
had been to spend the weekend with them at Winchelsea.

But the rest – his mother's soft cry, the sight of the monster
twisting incredibly across their path . . . was that the way it had been?
He had no way of knowing, no recollection of the time between
setting out from the house in Dulwich and waking in a hospital bed
with a nurse, young, dark and pretty, bending over and smiling and
telling him he was all right, and not to worry. He had wondered what
she was talking about, and asked what he was doing there; and she
had told him again not to worry about anything but to lie back and
rest, and he would have visitors very soon.

☐ Answer these questions without looking back.

1   Who is going to be the central character in the story?
2   What exactly has happened before the story begins?
3   What effect has it had on the central character?

☐ Now read the passage through again. If you have missed out anything important, add to your answers.

Section B   Winchelsea

☐ Read the passage through and follow the instructions at the end.

Neil walked through the crumbling stone archway into the empty
shell of what had been the nave of the church before it was destroyed
in the French wars. That was nearly seven hundred years ago.

Winchelsea then had been a thriving town, recently rebuilt here on its hill after the sea swallowed up old Winchelsea – like its sister-town, Rye, a brash newcomer to the company of the Cinque Ports and hopeful of outstripping its seniors in trade and prosperity. But the sea which destroyed the first port had capriciously moved away from the second, remaining as no more than a mocking gleam on the horizon.

So the hopes had come to nothing, and the traders had gone with the sea. Only a few squares were left of the grid pattern which had made the town a contemporary showplace of planning; and those were occupied by sleepy houses, fronted by lawns and flowers, three or four small shops, a couple of pubs. There had been no point in rebuilding the nave of the church, and the New Gate, which had marked the southern limits of Winchelsea, and through which one summer morning late in the thirteenth century the French had been treacherously admitted, stood now over a muddy lane, nearly a mile out in the country, surrounded by grazing sheep.

There were not many young people in Winchelsea. It was a place for retirement – that was why his grandparents had come to live in it. And in the past, although he had liked visiting them, Neil had felt a kind of impatience. Nothing happened here or was likely to happen, beyond the slow change of the seasons. He looked at the white facades of the houses making up the sides of the great square of the churchyard. Even the post-war ones had an appearance of having been there forever.

(It is often tempting to skip this kind of description. To do so, however, is usually a mistake, because the author has a good reason for including it. It gives us background *facts* and *atmosphere* to increase our understanding and enjoyment.)

1   List all the facts the author gives about the history of Winchelsea.
2   List the facts given about the appearance of the town.
3   Describe your impressions of what it would be like for someone of your age to live in.

Section C   In hospital

☐ Read the passage and then answer the questions that follow it.

He thought of the dream, and then of Grandpa coming to his bedside in the hospital. He had asked Neil how he was, and nodded when he said he had a headache.

'A touch of concussion, but they tell me you're sound in wind and limb.'

His grandfather, a Civil Servant until his retirement, was a tall thin man, with a long face lengthened further by a white pointed beard. Although he liked them both, Neil preferred him to his grandmother because he never fussed and talked directly, paying little regard to differences in age. His manner had always been calm and easy. He was trying to look calm and easy now, but not managing. Neil asked him:

'What happened?'

'What have they told you?'

'Nothing. I've not been awake long.'

'There was a smash. You don't remember it?'

His tone was even but Neil was conscious of the strain behind it. He thought of them all setting out together after lunch – Amanda insisting on going back to say another goodbye to Prinny, the cat, and worrying in case Mrs Redmayne might not remember to come in and feed him. . . . He said sharply:

'Where's Mummy? Is she in hospital, too?' He realized, for the first time properly, that the other beds in the ward were occupied by strangers. 'And Amanda, and Andy?'

'They're all right. Don't worry, Neil.'

There had been a hesitation, though; very slight, but enough to make the reassurance meaningless. And what he said was meaningless, anyway; because if they had been all right his mother would have been here, beside his bed. He said, hearing his voice echo as though far off:

'All of them?' He stared up at his grandfather. 'Dad, as well?'

'They're all right,' his grandfather repeated.

He did not need the sight of the tear rolling down the wrinkled cheek to give the lie. Nor did he resent it, knowing the lie was meant to help him, to ease him back into a world that had shattered and changed. But he could not go on looking at another human being. He turned and buried his head in the pillow, immobile, believing and not believing, while his grandfather's voice went on and on and he heard it without listening, an empty noise.

1 How did Neil get on with his grandfather?
2 How did the grandfather feel and why?
3 'He realized, for the first time properly, that the other beds in the ward were occupied by strangers.' Why was this important: what did it mean?
4 What does it normally mean when someone says, 'They're all right'?

50

5   What does it mean in this case?
6   Why does Neil's grandfather lie?

Section D   Writing

The author has now given the reader the facts and the atmosphere necessary to understand the story. Write one or two paragraphs explaining what you think those essential background facts and feelings are.

9 PENCIL AND PAPER GAMES

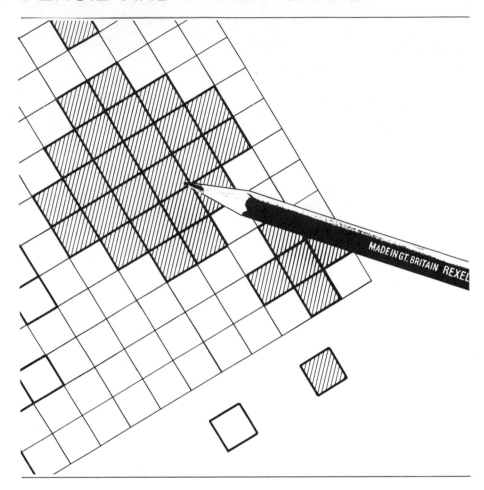

Section A Two word games

☐ Read the passage and follow the instructions at the end.

Acrostics

Acrostics is a word-building game. A word of at least three letters is chosen. Each player writes the word in a column down the left-hand side of a sheet of paper; he then writes the same word, but with the letters reversed, down the right-hand side of the page.

The player fills in the space between the two columns with the same number of words as there are letters in the keyword – and starting and ending each word with the letter at either side.

For example, if the keyword is 'stem,' a player's words might read: scream, trundle, earliest, manageress.

The winner may be either the first person to fill in all the words, or the player with the longest or most original words.

Transformation

Two words with the same number of letters are chosen. Each player writes down the two words. He tries to change the first word into the second word by altering only one letter at a time, and each time forming a new word.

For example, 'dog' could be changed to 'cat' in four words as follows: dog, cog, cot, cat. It is easiest to begin with three or four letter words until the players are quite practised – when five or even six letter words may be tried.

The winner is the player who completes the changes using the fewest number of words.

Pair work

1   Both choose one of these pairs for Acrostics. See who can complete the acrostics first.

       TAPE/EPAT   HELD/DLEH   SNARE/ERANS

2   Both choose one of these Transformations and see who can do it first:

      HEAT/COLD   HEAD/TAIL   EASY/HARD

Questions

3   Which of these is a correct answer in a game of Acrostics:

  a)   T A N   b) N OS E   c) Y EL P
       I SL E   O A T   A RI A
       N EA T   T ANG O   P RE Y
                        E ATI N

4   In Acrostics, how would you decide which of these players had won, if both finished at the same time?

  a)   N O W   b) N   ARRO   W
       E V E   E   XTENSIV   E
       W O N   W   OVE   N

5   Which of these is *not* a proper Transformation and why?

a)		b)		c)	
SNOW		DARK		DRY	
SLOW		DARE		WRY	
SLOT		FARE		WAY	
SLIT		FARR		WAN	
SLID		FAIR		WEN	
SAID				WET	
RAID					
RAIN					

☐ Read the passage and then follow the instructions at the end.

In this sophisticated pattern visualizing game, each player tries to form symmetrical shapes known as 'crystals'.

Equipment
All that is needed is a sheet of squared (graph) paper and as many differently coloured crayons as there are players.

The number of squares used for each game depends on the number of players: if two take part (the best number) about 20 rows of 20 squares each would form a suitable area.

Objective
Each player attempts to 'grow' crystals on the paper with the aim of filling more squares than his opponent.

A player does not score points for the number of crystals he grows, but for the number of squares his crystals cover.

Crystals
A crystal is made up of 'atoms', each of which occupies a single square. In growing crystals, players must observe certain rules of symmetry that determine whether or not a crystal is legitimate.

The symmetry of a crystal can be determined by visualizing four axes through its centre: horizontal, vertical, and two diagonal axes. Once the axes have been 'drawn', it should theoretically be possible to fold the crystal along each of the four axes to produce corresponding 'mirror' halves that, when folded, exactly overlay each other (i.e. are the same shape and size).

In addition to the rules of symmetry, players must observe the following:
  a) a legitimate crystal may be formed from four or more atoms drawn by one player only;
  b) the atoms forming a crystal must be joined along their sides – they may not be connected only by their corners;
  c) a crystal may not contain any empty atoms (i.e. holes).

Play
Players decide on their playing order and each one in turn shades in any one square of his choice – each player using a crayon of a different colour.

In their first few turns, players rarely try to grow a crystal. Instead, they place single atoms around the playing area in order to establish potential crystal sites. As play progresses, players will see which atoms are best placed for growing crystals and add to them as appropriate.

When a player thinks he has grown a crystal, he declares it, and rings the area that it covers.

A player with a winning advantage will try to retain the lead by either blocking his opponents' attempts at growing crystals, or by growing long narrow crystals that – although not high scoring – restrict the playing area.

Play ends when no blank squares are left, or when the players agree that no more crystals can be formed.

Scoring

Players work out which of the crystals are legitimate, and count the number of squares each crystal covers.

Any crystal that does not demonstrate symmetry around each of the four axes is not legitimate and does not score. The number of squares in the legitimate crystals that each player has grown are added, and the player with most squares wins the game.

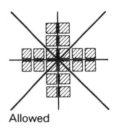

Disallowed

Allowed

Pair work

1 Play the game with a partner.

Questions

2 Which of these would be allowed as a crystal:

A
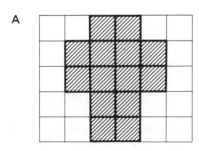

B
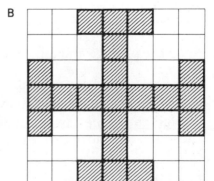

C
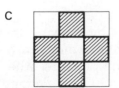

3   If this game stopped now, who would have won?

A = ▨   B = ☐

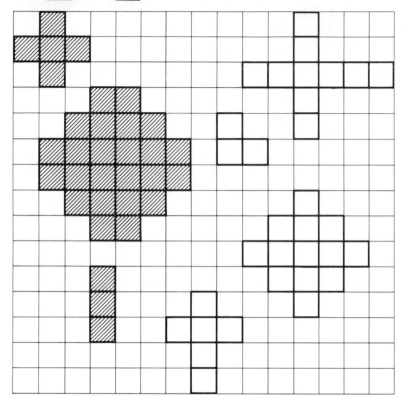

Section C   Aggression

☐ Read the passage and follow the instructions at the end.

Aggression is a game in which players fight imaginary battles in a bid to occupy the maximum amount of territory. Two players are ideal – though the game can also be played by three or more, who may choose to form teams. Each player must have a crayon of a different colour.

Playing area
A large sheet of paper is used. One player begins by drawing the boundaries of an imaginary country; each player in turn then draws the outline of an imaginary country adjoining one or more other countries. Any number of countries may be drawn (20 is an average

number if two play) and they can be any shape or size. When the agreed number of countries has been drawn, each is clearly marked with a different letter of the alphabet.

Armies

Each player is allotted 100 armies. Taking turns with his opponent, he chooses a country that he intends to occupy and writes within it how many armies he is allocating to it. (Once a country has been occupied, no player may add further armies to it.) This procedure continues until all the countries have been occupied, or until each player has allocated all his armies.

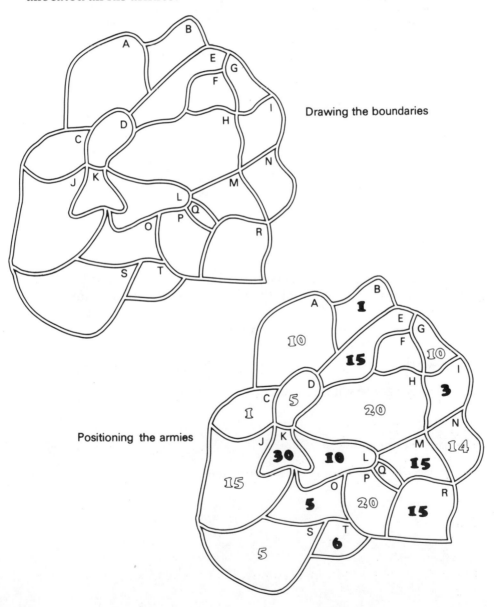

Drawing the boundaries

Positioning the armies

Play

The player who chose the first country has the opening move. His objective is to retain more occupied countries than his opponent; to achieve this he 'attacks' enemy armies in adjacent countries. (Adjacent countries are defined as those with a common boundary.) A player may attack with armies from more than one country – provided they are all in countries that have a common border with the country under attack.

If the number of armies located in the attacking country or countries is greater than those located in the defending country, the defending army is conquered – its armies are crossed off and can take no further part in the game. (The armies used to conquer a country may be re-used.) Players take it in turns to conquer countries until one or both of them cannot mount any further attacks.

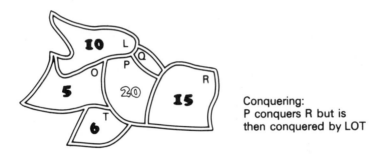

Conquering:
P conquers R but is
then conquered by LOT

Scoring

At the end of the game the players total the number of countries each of them retains. The winner is the player with the highest number of unconquered countries – he need not necessarily be the player who made the greatest number of conquests.

Pair work

1   Play the game with a partner.

Questions

2 Write labels to explain what is happening in this sequence of drawings from a game between *White* (4) and *Black* (**5**).

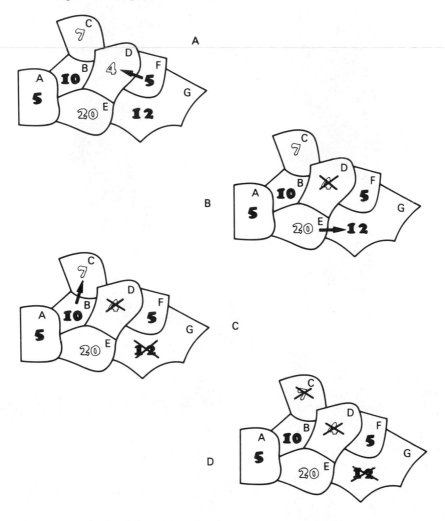

3 If you were *White* what would your next move be?

_____

Section D   Writing

_____

1 Which of the games in the unit did you find the most interesting to play, and why? Write a short paragraph explaining your views.
2 Choose another game (not necessarily a pencil and paper game) and explain the rules clearly and simply, following the pattern used in this unit.

10 JAMAICAN FRAGMENT

☐ The work in this unit should be tackled section by section. Do not read ahead.

☐ Follow the instructions, please.

Section A   A little incident

☐ Read the passage *once* only and then follow **Instructions** 1.

Every day I walk a half-mile from my home to the tramcar lines in the morning, and from the lines to my home in the evening. The walk is pleasant. The road on either side is flanked by red- and green-roofed bungalows, green lawns and gardens. The exercise is good for me and now and then I learn something from a little incident.

One morning, about halfway between my front gate and the tram track, I noticed two little boys playing in the garden of one of the more modest cottages. They were both very little boys, one was four years old perhaps, the other five. The bigger of the two was a sturdy youngster, very dark, with a mat of coarse hair on his head and coal-black eyes. He was definitely a little Jamaican – a strong little Jamaican. The other little fellow was smaller, but also sturdy – he was white, with hazel eyes and light-brown hair. Both were dressed in blue shirts and khaki pants: they wore no shoes and their feet were muddy. They were not conscious of my standing there watching them; they played on. The game, if it could be called a game, was not elaborate. The little white boy strode imperiously up and down and every now and then shouted imperiously at his bigger playmate. The little brown boy shuffled along quietly behind him and did what he was told.

'Pick up that stick!' The dark boy picked it up.

'Jump into the flowers!' The dark boy jumped.

'Get me some water!' The dark boy ran inside. The white boy sat down on the lawn.

I was amazed. Here before my eyes, a white baby, for they were little more than babies, was imposing his will upon a little black boy. And the little black boy submitted. I puzzled within myself as I went down the road. Could it be that the little dark boy was the son of a servant in the home and therefore had to do the white boy's bidding? No. They were obviously dressed alike, the little dark boy was of equal class with his playmate. No. They were playmates, the little dark boy was a neighbour's child. I was sure of that. Then how was it that he obeyed so faithfully the white boy's orders? Was it that even at his early age he sensed that in his own country he would be at the white man's beck and call? Could he in such youth divine a difference between himself and the white boy? And did the little white youngster so young, such a baby, realize that he would grow to dominate the black man? Was there an indefinable quality in the white man that enabled his baby, smaller and younger than his playmate, to make him his slave? Was there really some difference between a white man and a black man? Something that made the white superior? I could find no answer. I could not bring myself to believe such a thing, and yet, with my own eyes I had seen a little dark boy take orders from a little white boy – a little white boy obviously his social equal, and younger and smaller. Were we as a race really inferior? So inferior that even in our infancy we realized our deficiencies, and accepted a position as the white man's servant?

For a whole day I puzzled over this problem. For a whole day my faith in my people was shaken. When I passed that afternoon the little boys were not there. That evening I thought deeply on the subject.

Instructions

1 **Without looking back at the passage** write out the main points of
the story from memory. Number them and start like this:
   1 He was walking from his home to the tramcar lines.
   2 He saw two boys playing in a garden.
   3
2 **Now read the passage again.** Check your version and correct any
serious mistakes, but do not add a lot of details.
3 What colour is the author? How do you know?
4 Briefly describe the two boys.
5 Explain in a few sentences of your own what they were doing.
6 How did the author *feel* about this?
7 The last part of the passage describes his *thoughts*. He asked
himself, 'How was it that he obeyed so faithfully the white boy's
orders?' In a few sentences of your own explain the thoughts that
went through his head in answer to that question.

Section B   A surprise

☐ Read the passage and then answer the question that follows it.
DO NOT READ AHEAD

The next morning the boys were there again, and a man was
standing at the gate watching them. I stopped and looked, just to see
what the white boy was making his little servant do. To my utter
astonishment the little dark boy was striding imperiously up and
down the lawn, while the white youngster walked abjectly behind
him.
'Get me a banana!' The little white boy ran into the house and
reappeared shortly with a banana. 'Peel it for me!' The little white boy
skinned the banana and handed it to his dark master.
I saw it now.

☐ Explain in your own words what it was that he 'saw'. What was going
on?

Section C   I explain

In this section ten words have been missed out.

☐ Read the passage and work out suitable words to fill the spaces.

- [ ] Write the number of each space and beside it the word you have chosen.

- [ ] Then follow the instruction at the end.
  DO NOT READ AHEAD

This was indeed a game, a game I had played as a child. Each boy took it in turn every — 1 — day to be the boss, the other the slave. It had been great fun to me as a youngster. I smiled as I — 2 —. I looked at the man standing by the gate. He was a white man. I remembered what I had thought yesterday. He, no — 3 —, I thought to myself, was wondering if the black race is superior to the white. I laughed — 4 — to myself. How silly grown-ups are, how clever we are, how wonderfully able we are to impute deep motives to childish actions! How — 5 — we are when we have been warped by prejudice! This man, I said to myself, will — 6 — all day on whether the blacks will eventually arise and rule the world because he thinks he sees a little black boy realizing at a — 7 — age his superiority over the white. I will save him his puzzle. I will explain it to him. I went across to him.

'I know what you're thinking,' I said. 'You're thinking that maybe the black race is — 8 — to the white, because you just saw the little dark youngster on the lawn ordering the little white boy around. Don't think that, it's a game they play. Alternate days one is — 9 —, the other the servant. It's a grand game. I used to play it and maybe so did you. Yesterday I saw the little white boy bossing the dark one and worried all day over the dark boy's — 10 — of his inferiority so young in life! We are silly, we grown-ups, aren't we?'

Instruction

The next sentence in the story is this:
   'The man was surprised at my outburst.'
The remaining sentences go on to explain why he was surprised and how he managed to give the author a surprise. What further twist can the story have? Think about this.

- [ ] Write your own ending to the story.

Section D   This is Jamaica

- [ ] Read the passage and then answer the question at the end.

The man was surprised at my outburst. He looked at me smiling.

63

'I know all about the game,' he said. 'The boys are brothers – my sons.' He pointed to a handsome brown woman on the veranda who had just come out to call in the children. 'That's my wife,' he said.

I smiled. My spirit laughed within me. This is Jamaica, I said in my heart, this is my country – my people. I looked at the white man. He smiled at me. 'We'll miss the tram if we don't hurry,' he said.

☐ Can you think of a better title for this story? Try to think of a title that sums up for you what the story is about.

11 THE PISTOL

This unit is different from most of the others in the book, because it is not divided into sections. Instead you are asked to look at the text as a whole. It comes from an autobiography by Christopher Milne, the son of A. A. Milne, creator of Winnie the Pooh.

☐ Read the text through once and then study the instructions at the end. They will suggest ways in which you should reread it.

1   Once when a friend of my parents was lunching with us, she asked what I did with myself all day. My father answered for me that I spent a lot of my time just wandering about.
    'You let him go where he likes?'
    'Yes.'
    'You're not afraid he might get into danger?'
    'No. He knows how to look after himself.'

2   There are a hundred ways in which a boy can injure – if not indeed kill – himself. The more adventurous he is and the greater his initiative, the more ways he will find. If you protect him from each of the hundred, he is sure to find the hundred and first. Though most men can look back on their boyhood and tremble at the narrowness of some of their escapes, most boys do in fact survive more or less intact, and the wise father is the trusting father. My father's trust was so natural that I never thought about it or about the anxiety that must often have lain behind it. Take the following story, for instance: the story of my pistol.

3   One day Robin and I (Robin was a friend of mine: we were both about nine years old at the time) were playing in the gardens outside the Natural History Museum in London when we became aware of another boy who was engaged in firing a pistol. It was the sound that attracted our attention. For it was not the feeble popping of a cap pistol, but an ear-splitting explosion – quite the real thing. We went over to him to get a closer look. He fired again: it was most impressive. We asked him if we could see it, and proudly he showed it to us. We asked where he had bought it, and he told us.

4   Robin had the sort of parents who don't usually say no. So it was agreed that he should put the matter to them. And shortly afterwards the two pistols were produced and two boxes of blank cartridges, one for each of us. To try them out I was invited to Richmond Park; and while Robin's mother sat on the grass surrounded by the remains of our picnic, he and I battled with his father over a fallen tree trunk. Afterwards his father said: 'If those had been real pistols I'd have been riddled with bullets through and through.' Riddled with bullets: what wonderful, memorable words.

5   A year or two later, at Cotchford, I was looking at my pistol, still as beloved as ever. It was small and simple, but well and solidly and safely made. You could fire it point blank at an enemy without too much risk because it discharged downwards through a hole in the underside of the barrel near its tip. The tip itself was blocked. So you couldn't in fact load it with anything other than blank cartridges, which was a pity – unless, of course, you filed the tip off. I had a file, and set to work.

6   The file cut through the metal quite easily and soon the job was done and the end smoothed off. Then I loaded with a blank cartridge and pushed three or four gimp pins down the barrel. The cupboard where I kept my tools would do for a target. I stood a yard or two away and pulled the trigger. The noise indoors was deafening. I looked at the cupboard and was pleased to see that it was nicely riddled with gimp pins. This was a satisfactory start. The next step was to see about getting some better cartridges, cartridges with bullets.

7   My contact for this sort of thing was Mitchell's Garage. The two brothers who ran it – one fat, one thin – were useful allies. For without some sort of help I was a bit stuck: both Tunbridge Wells and East Grinstead being beyond my range. So a message was passed to Mitchell's – probably via Mrs Wilson – and eventually (oh, wonderful day!) a message came back that the cartridges awaited my collection. I put my pistol in my pocket, called for Pat (Mrs Wilson's daughter) and together we set off up the lane.

8   Mitchell's Garage was a large, barn-like structure with room for lots of cars inside it, but on this occasion it was more or less empty. The cartridges looked fine, with round, lead bullets sticking out of their ends. I stood in the middle of the garage and loaded. I had a bit of difficulty getting the cartridge to go right in: it went most of the way, then jammed. But by slightly loosening a screw I was able to get the breech mechanism to close behind it. Then I pulled the trigger. There was a loud explosion, an alarming flash and a violent stinging sensation in my hand. I dropped the pistol with a cry and found the back of my hand spattered with gunpowder and blood. Luckily the damage was not serious and I turned my attention to the pistol. What had gone wrong? At once I saw. The hole in the barrel was not big enough. That was why I had been unable to push the cartridge in properly in the first place. I ought to have seen this at the time. The bullet had stuck and the explosion backfired. Tragedy! I took the pistol to Mr Mitchell. What could he do? Was it possible to drill out the barrel? He looked at it, said he thought it was, and together we went into his workshop. With the barrel drilled out, the cartridges fitted perfectly and I was all set to try another shot then and there, but rather to my surprise Mr Mitchell said 'No, no. Please! Not here!' and hurried me outside. So I kept my first shot for a gate on the way home that had a notice on it saying 'Private'.

9   The pistol now worked beautifully and I could fire it at all sorts of things, though only at inanimate things. Neither my father nor I ever took any pleasure in killing, and hated those who did. So mostly I aimed at trees and sometimes I let Pat aim too, and once I even allowed my father to aim. I aimed and usually I missed. The pistol wasn't as accurate as I had hoped. Perhaps it needed sights. So I made a foresight and a backsight with bits of wire twisted round the barrel and then glued. Then I found an old plywood target and took it down to the river and hung it from a branch of the oak tree. I fired, expecting the target to be knocked sideways by the impact, but nothing happened. Had I missed? I went closer and fired again. Again nothing. This was very disappointing. My sights must be wrong. I went still closer . . . and then I saw the two neat holes going clean through the plywood, and I was thrilled.

10   So that was my pistol, and for a year or two it gave me immense

pleasure. Then one day at breakfast my father said: 'Do you remember John Wetherell? I've just heard from his father that he's lost an eye. He was playing with a gun and it went off in his face.' An awful, icy feeling hit me in the stomach. John was a boy I used to play cricket with, a wonderful batsman, one of my heroes. 'He *could* go on playing cricket, of course. You *can* play cricket with only one eye. Ranji did, as you know. But his father has thrown in his hand, doesn't want him ever to play again.' A pause while this awful story sank in and spread its message throughout my entire body, down into my feet and into the tips of my fingers. Then, very gently my father added: 'That's why I've never been too happy about your pistol.'

11   Nothing more was said or needed to be said. After breakfast I put pistol, box of cartridges and a screwdriver into my pocket and went down to the river. I chose a place where the water was deepest. I threw the cartridges in first, one at a time, scattering them here and there over the surface of the water. Then with the screwdriver I took my pistol to bits. There were five pieces, and, walking down the river bank, I chose five separate places for them, so that they could never come together again, threw them in, watched them sink.

12   Then I came home.

Structure

1   Paragraphs 1, 2, 3, and 4 can be divided into two main sections of the story. These could be entitled:
        Introduction: a father's trust
        I get my starting pistol.
    How would you divide those first 35 lines to fit these titles?
2   The remainder of the story can be divided into three main sections. How would you divide it up? What titles would you give to the three sections?
3   The story takes place at different times. Sometimes a rough measurement of time is given. At others, the author simply puts 'one day', or a similar phrase. Divide the story into its main *time* divisions – these are not necessarily the same as the sections used before, since there are more of them. For each one write any indication the author gives of when these events took place.

Some details

4   The biggest story section is covered by paragraphs 5, 6, 7, and 8. Read them again carefully and sort out the main events that happened. List them as a series of separate events like this:
    1   He examined the pistol and realized what had to be done to make it fire.
    2   He got a file and began to file the tip.

5 Draw a diagram of the pistol as it was. Show, by your drawing, what the author did to it to make it fire. This was in two stages, so you may need to make more than one drawing.

Interpreting the story

6 Retell the story of paragraphs 7 and 8 in the form of a *script*. Start like this:

(CHRISTOPHER *is in his room, cleaning his pistol, when* MRS WILSON *comes in.*)

CHRISTOPHER: Hallo Mrs Wilson. Have you heard from Mitchell's yet?

MRS WILSON: Yes. I got a message this morning saying they've got the cartridges and will you go down there and collect them.

7 Imagine that you are a journalist. You have been sent to interview the famous author A. A. Milne. You have heard that he has some unusual ideas about how to bring up a son. Write the interview you have with him about this. (Use the details given in this story in your interview.)

12 BULLFIGHT

Before you start work on Section A, write down, briefly, your feelings about bullfighting.

Section A   A doubtful beginning

☐ Read the passage and then answer the questions at the end.

1   We arrived late to find the gates of the bull-ring locked and a large crowd struggling among a squad of mounted police. A man with a megaphone told them to go home, that the corrida had begun and the ring was full. We were just on the point of turning away when a party of gold-braided officers arrived, we fell in behind them, doors were thrown open, officials saluted us, and in no time at all we found ourselves ushered into a private box high above the arena.

2   Before us lay the classic scene: the ring of sand, the crescent of sunlight, the banked circle of spectators with dark-blue faces like flints in a wall, and the two almost motionless antagonists below us – the bull-fighter with bowed head, standing in silence; and coughing in the dust, a young bull dying.

3   We had arrived at the second kill of the afternoon; but we saw four more, the best and the worst – the best magnificent, the worst a crime. In a corrida of this nature one may see anything. The young toreros, eager to establish names for themselves, are often capable of a feverish bravado, but more often suffer from a kind of hysteria which loses them control of both bull and themselves. The bulls, too, are often a green, unpredictable lot, capable of nobility, treachery and excruciating cowardice. Not rarely, in such circumstances, the boy gets killed as well as the bull.

4   The second bull that afternoon seemed to have been killed with some skill, for as the boy stood there with his blood-stained sword, he received no groans or hisses. A quartet of plumed horses dragged away the body, the sand was raked smooth, and we waited for the entry of the next. This is one of the great dramatic moments of every encounter; the fighters take up their positions, the hushed crowd waits, then the huge doors to the bull-pit are thrown open and the unknown beast charges forth, fresh in anger, into the ring.

5   The trumpet for our third bull duly sounded, the doors were thrown open, the attendant scampered for safety, and we all waited; but nothing happened at all. The attendant crept back and peered cautiously round the corner of the open doorway. He whistled and waved his cap. Then, gaining courage, he began to leap up and down in the mouth of the bull-pit, hooting and capering like a clown. Minutes passed, and still nothing happened. Slowly, at last, and sadly, lost as a young calf, the bull walked into the ring. He looked with bewilderment around him, turned back, found the doors shut and began to graze in the sand. If ever a body lacked a vocation for martyrdom, this sorry bull was it. He had no conception of what was expected of him, nor any inborn anger; all he wished was to be back in the brown pastures under Medina and to have no part of this. And when it came to the point, he put up no fight at all and was killed at last without grace or honour, to the loud derision of the crowd.

The main points

1   This section consists of five paragraphs. Look at them again and decide what is the main subject matter of each one. Write one sentence for each paragraph, summing up its subject matter.
2   In one or two of your own sentences explain why the writer was lucky to get into the bullfight at all, and how he did it.

3 Why was it difficult for him to know whether the fights he was going to see would be good or bad?
4 Why was the third bull a disappointment?

The details

5 Describe in your own words what the writer could see when he first looked down into the arena.
6 In what ways are the toreros and bulls similar to each other 'in a corrida of this nature'?
7 What happens between the death of one bull and the arrival of the next?
8 Why did the attendant 'leap up and down in the mouth of the bull-pit'?

Vocabulary

9 Find each of these words in the passage. Write down what you think it means. If you are not sure, try to work it out from the way it is used.
    ushered   antagonists   corrida   green   derision

Section B   Gloria's champion

In this section twelve words have been missed out. They are listed, in the wrong order, at the end.

☐ Work out which word should go in which space.

☐ Write the number of each space and against it write the word you have chosen.

   Every corrida is run by a President, the formal — 1 — who commands the various stages of the ritual, and his box stood next to ours. It was the centre of honour and dedication, to which each torero bowed at the beginning and end of his — 2 —. And this afternoon it was decorated by the presence of four young girls all dressed in the handsome robes of fiesta. White lace mantillas clothed their heads, and over their shoulders they wore rich black shawls embroidered with scarlet flowers. They leaned their bare brown arms on the parapet, and — 3 —, and turned every so often to flash their teeth at the solemn gentlemen who stood sipping — 4 — behind them. Silly, self-conscious, but undeniably beautiful, they were not spectators but symbols, the virgins of the feast, flower-soft among the blood, providing that contrast of youth and death so beloved by every —5 —.

A superb, straight-limbed young man now stepped forward into the — 6 — and a cheer went up, for he had already earned some — 7 —. He was dressed, not in the heavy gold-embroidered garments of the professional matador, but in Andalusian riding-clothes – a broad black hat, short waistcoat, tight-fitting trousers and high-heeled boots. With cape folded, hat held to his breast, he faced the President's box, bowed, raised his head, and in ringing — 8 — tones dedicated the next bull to one of the virgins, whose name was Gloria. Her companions congratulated her rather noisily upon the honour, while she, huge-eyed and — 9 — as a doll, waved a small hand, and then went pale as death.

The President leaned forward and gave the signal, the trumpet — 10 —, and the doors opened for the fourth bull. And this time there was no doubt about it. He came in like — 11 —, snorting and kicking up the dust, his black coat shining like a seal's, his horned head lowered for immediate attack. Two assistants, trailing long capes, ran out and played him first, a formal prologue designed to discover the unknown — 12 — of the bull, his way of charging, which horn he liked using, and so on. Slowly, their job done, they were beaten back towards the barriers, and the bull stood alone.

sherries   ring   trial   eloquent   figurehead   delicate   sounded chattered   thunder   reputation   Spaniard   temper

---

Section C   The death

This section has been divided into nine parts. Except for the first part, they have been printed in the wrong order.

☐ Read them through and work out the correct order.

☐ Write the numbers in that order.

Then Gloria's champion walked out across the sand. He took up his stand, the pale sun gilding his rigid face, gave a loud clear shout to the bull, and from that moment we witnessed an almost faultless combat.

1   The boy, sword in hand, faced the panting bull. They stood at close range, eyeing each other in silence. The bull lowered his head, and the crowd roared 'Now!'

2　But the boy's sword had found its mark, and the bull folded his legs, lay down for a moment as though resting at pasture, then slowly rolled over and died.

　　The crowd rose to its feet with one loud cry. Hats, caps, cushions, even raincoats, were thrown into the ring.

3　Elegant, firm-footed as a dancer, but with cold courage and movements of continual beauty, the boy entirely dominated the bull. He seemed to turn the fury of the beast into a creative force which he alone controlled, a thrusting weight of flesh and bone with which he drew ritual patterns across the sand.

4　His undefended body, poised thus above the horns, is so vulnerable that a flick of the bull's head could disembowel him. It is the moment of truth, when only courage, skill and a kind of blind faith can preserve the fighter's life.

5　The young man stood among these tributes and smiled palely at the crowd. Then he came, sword in hand, and bowed low to the President and to Gloria. Colour and intoxication had returned to the girl's cheeks; she stood up and clapped him wildly and threw him a box of cigars. His triumph was hers; it was the least she could do.

6　He never ran, he scarcely moved his feet, but he turned his cape like liquid fire, and the bull, snorting with mysterious amazement, seemed to adore him against his will, brushing the cape as a bee does a poppy.

　　After the short barbed lances had been thrust into the bull's shoulders, drawing their threads of blood, the moment for the kill arrived; and this was accomplished with almost tragic simplicity and grace.

7　The boy raised the sword slowly to his eye, aiming horizontally along the blade; then he leaned far forward and plunged the weapon to the hilt in the bull's black heaving shoulders. Such a moment, the climax in the game, carries with it mortal danger for the matador.

8 The bull charged and charged again, loud-nostrilled, sweating for death, and the boy turned and teased him at will, reducing him at last to a kind of enchanted helplessness, so that the bull stood hypnotized, unable to move, while the young man kissed his horns. Alone in the ring, unarmed with the armed beast, he had proved himself the stronger.

Section D   Writing

Look at what you wrote before you started work on Section A. In what ways has reading the chapter affected your views? Has it confirmed them, or altered them? Write a paragraph in answer to these questions.

13 CHARRADA

Section A   The void

☐ Read the passage and follow the instructions at the end.

At Dynmouth Comprehensive Timothy Gedge found no subject interesting. Questioned some years ago by the headmaster, a Mr Stringer, he had confessed to this and Mr Stringer had stirred his coffee and said it was a bad thing. He'd asked Timothy what he found interesting outside the Comprehensive and Timothy had said television shows. Prompted further by Mr Stringer, he'd confessed that as soon as he walked into the empty flat on his return from school he turned on the television and was always pleased to watch whatever there was. Sitting in a room with the curtains drawn, he delighted in hospital dramas and life at the Crossroads Motel and horse-racing and cookery demonstrations. In the holidays there were the morning programmes as well: Bagpuss, Camp Runamuck, *Nai Zindagi Naya Jeevan*, Funky Phantom, Randall and Hopkirk (deceased), Junior

Police Five, Car Body Maintenance, Solids, Liquids and Gases, Play a Tune with Ulf Goran, Sheep Production. Mr Stringer said it was a bad thing to watch so much television. 'I suppose you'll go into the sandpaper factory?' he'd suggested and Timothy had replied that it seemed the best bet. On the school notice-board a sign permanently requested recruits for a variety of departments in the sandpaper factory. He'd been eleven or twelve when he'd first assumed that that was where his future lay.

But then, not long after this conversation with Mr Stringer, an extraordinary thing happened. A student teacher called O'Hennessy arrived at the Comprehensive and talked to his pupils about a void when he was scheduled to be teaching them English. 'The void can be filled,' he said.

Nobody paid much attention to O'Hennessy, who liked to be known by his Christian name, which was Brehon. Nobody under-stood a word he was talking about. 'The landscape is the void,' he said. 'Escape from the drear landscape. Fill the void with beauty.' All during his English classes Brehon O'Hennessy talked about the void, and the drear landscape, and beauty. In every kid, he pronounced, looking from one face to another, there was an avenue to a fuller life. He had a short tangled beard and tangled black hair. He had a way of gesturing in the air with his right hand, towards the windows of the classroom. 'There,' he said when he did this. 'Out there. The souls of the adult people have shrivelled away: they are as last year's rhubarb walking the streets. Only the void is left. Get up in the morning, take food, go to work, take food, work, go home, take food, look at the television, go to bed, have sex, go to sleep, get up.' Now and again during his lessons he smoked cigarettes containing the drug cannabis and didn't mind if his pupils smoked also, cannabis or tobacco, who could care? 'Your soul is your property,' he said.

Timothy Gedge, like all the others, had considered O'Hennessy to be touched in the head, but then O'Hennessy said something that made him less certain about that. Everyone was good at something, he said, nobody was without talent: it was a question of discovering yourself. O'Hennessy was at the Comprehensive for only half a term, and was then replaced by Miss Wilkinson.

Research

The passage refers to three characters:
   Timothy Gedge
   Mr Stringer
   Brehon O'Hennessy
Read it through again and list all the information you can find about each character's appearance and personality.

Questions

Now answer these questions in writing:
1 What kind of person do you think Timothy was?
2 What did Brehon O'Hennessy look like?
3 Do you get any impression of what Mr Stringer was like? If so, what is it?

Writing

Continue the following conversation.

O'HENNESSY: I've been talking to 3A about their ambitions.
STRINGER: I don't know about their ambitions, but I can tell you what their futures are.
O'HENNESSY: Can you?
STRINGER: Yes – leave school, go into the sandpaper factory, get married, raise a family . . .
O'HENNESSY:

Section B Charades

This section has been divided into eight parts. Except for the first they have been printed in the wrong order.

☐ Read them through and work out the correct order.

☐ Write the numbers in that order.

It seemed to Timothy that he was good at nothing, but he also was increasingly beginning to wonder if he wished to spend a lifetime making sandpaper. He thought about himself, as Brehon O'Hennessy had said he should. He closed his eyes and saw himself, again following Brehon O'Hennessy's injunction.

1 Timothy laughed himself, seeing in a mirror how peculiar he looked, with a pair of tights stuffed into the dress to give him a bosom. He enjoyed laughing at himself and being laughed at. He enjoyed the feel of the wig on his head and the different feeling the long voluminous dress gave him, turning him into another person.

2   She called it a game. 'The game of charades,' she said. '*Charrada*. From
    the Spanish, the chatter of the clown.' She divided 3A into five groups
    and gave each an historical incident to act. The others had to guess
    what it was. Nobody had listened when she'd said that the word
    came from the Spanish and meant the chatter of a clown; within five
    minutes the classroom was a bedlam.

3   He saw himself as an adult, getting up in the morning and taking
    food, and then reporting to the cutting room of the sandpaper
    factory. Seeking to discover an absorbing interest, which might even
    become an avenue to a fuller life, he bought a model-aeroplane kit,
    but unfortunately he found the construction work difficult. The balsa
    wood kept splitting and the recommended glue didn't seem to stick
    the pieces together properly.

4   It was the only occasion he had ever enjoyed at Dynmouth Compre-
    hensive and it was crowned by his discovery that without any
    difficulty whatsoever he could adopt a falsetto voice. That night he'd
    lain awake in bed, imagining a future that was different in every way
    from a future in the sandpaper factory. '*Charrada*,' Miss Wilkinson
    repeated in a dream. 'The chatter of the clown.'

5   He lost some of them, and after a couple of days he gave the whole
    thing up. It was a great disappointment to him. He'd imagined flying
    the clever little plane on the beach, getting the engine going and
    showing people how it was done. He'd imagined making other
    aircraft, building up quite a collection of them, using dope like it said
    in the instructions, covering the wings with tissue paper.

6   It would all have taken hours, sitting contentedly in the kitchen with
    the radio on while his mother and sister were out in the evenings, as
    they generally were. But it was not to be.
        Then, on the afternoon of December 4th last, something else
    happened: Miss Wilkinson ordered that the two laundry baskets
    containing the school's dressing-up clothes should be carried into the
    classroom and she made the whole of 3A dress up so that they could
    enact scenes from history.

7   The eight children in Timothy Gedge's group laughed uproariously
    when he dressed up as Queen Elizabeth I, in a red wig and a garment
    that had a lank white ruff at its neck.

In this section four sentences have been missed out. The gaps where
they should go have been closed up. The missing sentences are listed
at the end of the passage in the correct order.

☐ Work out where the sentences should go.

He'd felt aimless in his adolescence before that. After he'd failed with
the model aeroplane kit he'd taken to following people about just to
see where they were going, and looking through the windows of
people's houses. He continued to follow people about and to look
5 through windows and to attend funerals, but he had also determined
to enter the Spot the Talent competition at the Easter Fête with a
comic act and he now spent a considerable amount of his spare time
trying to work out what it should be. He instinctively felt that
somehow it should incorporate the notion of death, that whatever
10 *charrada* he devised should be of a macabre nature.
    In bed at night he thought about this, and continued to do so
during geography lessons and tedious mathematics lessons, staring
ahead of him in a manner that was complained of as vacant. He would
smile when he was insulted in this way and for a moment would pay
15 attention to a droning voice retailing information about the distri-
bution of herring-beds around the shores of the British Isles or in-
comprehensibly speaking French. He wondered about presenting
himself as a female mourner, in a black dress down to his feet and a
veiled black hat, with cheekily relevant chatter. But somehow that
20 didn't seem complete, or even right. At half-past eleven that morning Timothy Gedge had found the solution he was looking for: he
decided to base his comic act on the deaths of Miss Munday, Mrs
Burnham and Miss Lofty, the Brides in the Bath, the victims of George
Joseph Smith. To applause and laughter in the marquee at the Easter
25 Fête, he rose from an old tin bath while the limelight settled on the
wedding-dress he wore and his chatter began. He'd never in his life
seen Benny Hill, or anyone else, attempting an act in a long white
wedding-dress, impersonating three deceased women. It made him
chortle so much in the coach that Mr Stringer asked him if he was
30 going to be sick.

a) He'd found himself regularly attending funerals because for
    some reason there was enjoyment of a kind to be derived from
    standing in the graveyard of the church of St Simon and St Jude
    or the graveyard of the Baptist, Methodist or Catholic churches,
    while solemn words were said and mourners paid respects.

b) He would then revert to his more personal riddle of how to reconcile death and comedy in a theatrical act.

c) Then, a month ago, Mr Stringer had taken forty pupils to London and had included in the itinerary a visit to Madame Tussaud's.

d) All the way back to Dynmouth on the coach he'd imagined the act.

Section D Writing

Imagine you are Mr Stringer. You have to write a detailed report on Timothy's progress and development over the year. What would you write?

14 GO PLAY BUTTERFLY

Section A How it happened

___

☐ Read the passage and then follow the instructions at the end.

'I'll fix you to fly away,' the young man said. Then he asked Esther to
hold still while he pinned on her wings. It was two nights before the
Carnival, and Esther was aglow with the importance of it.

    She hadn't wanted to do it at first. She didn't even know what
Carnival was, but her mother had decided for her. Josephine, her
friend from school, and Carol, who lived down the road, were both
Trinidadians, and their mums had decided that they would 'play'
with a band. Carol had boasted about her costume in the presence of
Esther's mum. It was too much of a challenge. Esther knew that her
mother would pick up the gauntlet and that she would be made to
'play mas*' too.

    Carol's family were moving. Her mother, who came and gos-

mas is short for masquerade

sipped with Esther's mother, told endless stories about the beauty of their new house in Norwood. Everything she said implied that they'd finished with Brixton, finished with living in a council flat. They were home owners now. There were to be lace curtains and a new colour telly and a fence which was to be painted pink, and a bedroom for Carol and one for Stanley and one for the twins, and a dining-room which was separate from the kitchen. It was too much for Esther's mother, Mistress Waters, to take. And now Carol was in a band which was going to have its photograph in the *South London Press*, her mum said.

When Manny came home, Mistress Waters questioned him closely. What was all this Carnival business? Couldn't Esther take part in it if they wanted her to? Manny said he knew Soaky who was the artistic director of one of the 'mas camps'; he could get her in, even at this late date, no problem. Manny was Esther's stepfather. She liked him. He knew everyone. He took her to the mas camp the next day. Esther could see that at first he wasn't too taken by the idea, but her mum had said it must be so, and it was.

The camp was a huge disused factory in Paddington. Manny drove Esther there and left her with his friend Soaky, a man with greying temples and a long straight nose, strange on the face of a black man. Esther was uncomfortable. Soaky's real name was Mr Dix, but all the kids in the camp called him Soaky. So Esther called him Soaky too. As soon as they walked in through the factory doors, a little gate, hinged into a larger one, Esther began to feel that sense of wanting to be anywhere but there. It was a place which would challenge her. It was a hive of activity. There were young men and women, most of them much older than Esther, working away at the trestles and the nylon and the tinsel, at tables all over the large and disorderly room. They didn't look up from their work when she came in with Manny, who sought Soaky out and introduced his daughter.

This is the beginning of a story. The author has a lot of information to tell us so that we understand and enjoy the story. Much of it is in this first section. These instructions suggest ways of making sure that you have understood all the necessary facts.

1   Make a list of all the *characters* mentioned. Beside each one write a brief description of who he or she is.
2   Make a numbered list of the main *events* in the story. Put them in the order in which they happened, like this:

   1. Carol's mother kept boasting about the new house they were moving to.
   2. She boasted, too, that Carol was playing with a band.

3 Mistress Waters, Esther and Manny all had different attitudes to the Carnival and the people taking part in it. In one or two sentences per person sum up these attitudes.
4 Write a paragraph of not more than 75 words summing up this part of the story. Write it like the *'New readers begin here'* piece at the start of a magazine serial episode.

Section B   Fantasia of the Ethereal Air

In this section seven sentences have been missed out. They are listed at the end of the passage in the wrong order.

☐ Read the passage and work out where the sentences should go.

☐ Write the number of each space and beside it write the letter of the sentence you have chosen.

Soon, Manny became enthusiastic about the mas camp. He liked to take the drive to Paddington, and would volunteer to take Esther there. He began speaking about the camp as though it was his own enterprise. ——————— 1 ——————— He would plant her in the camp and go off for a few hours, making his rounds in 'the Grove', and hanging around the betting shops of Notting Hill. He would come back to pick her up, elevated or exhausted with the tensions of placing money on a horse.

——————— 2 ——————— He called out to a group of youths who were busy painting the stretched fabric of the dresses that the players would wear. Their band was called 'Fantasia of the Ethereal Air'. Soaky took Esther round to the youths and said, 'Give this girl some wings; she go play butterfly.'

The young men, four of them, were sizing Esther up. ——————— 3 ——————— Another of them said they were going to make her 'high, high' and asked her if a man had ever made her feel so light and airborne before. Esther was only fourteen. Men didn't speak to her like that. ——————— 4 ——————— She kissed her teeth and turned her head away, pretending to look at the group of girls who were kneeling round another masquerader, pinning a costume on her with safety pins and needles clasped in their teeth. Esther moved away from Jojo and Claude and the rest of them and joined the group of women who were dyeing feathers.

From the day she had come there she had sensed that they had all treated her like she had never been treated before. ——————— 5 ——————— Manny had told Soaky that she was only fourteen, and the boys had said that she was 'fit' and Manny had looked at them as though to say they'd gone too far. ———— 6 ———— It was the first time that she'd been made self-conscious by a group of boys about her body. It was not only the way they looked it up and down, not only the way their eyes seemed to say that she had some magnetism. ———— 7 ———— And the other stars were women much older than herself, girls who swirled in and out of the camp and were attended with the respect due to beauty, to flourish, to independence. Esther was happy to be in that team, amongst the forty women who were to play mas with Fantasia.

a)   On their second visit to the camp, Soaky had asked Esther to help make the costumes.

b)   It was also the first time that she was going to be one of the stars.

c)   At least, she hadn't known them to before then.

d)   Esther knew that he was eager to carry* her because it enabled him to get away from her mother.

e)   That's what they made her feel, Esther thought, older than herself.

f)   One of them was called Jojo, and he smiled at her.

g)   Jojo and his mob had made remarks about her size.

*carry means 'take' or 'give a lift to someone' in Trinidadian dialect.

Section C   Carnival Queen

☐ Read the passage and then answer the questions at the end.

Twice when Esther had been there, the star of their band had walked into the mas camp. Esther thought she was gorgeous. She had an imperial look; a black beauty with a touch of disdain on her face. Esther knew that she was called Veronica. Soaky spoke of her as his leading lady. She stood at the door like someone who owned the place but still wanted to be treated like a visiting queen. The camp gathered round her when she walked in and held out her arms to be measured finally for the draperies that were to envelop them. She held back her head when Soaky and an assistant lifted the head-dress, peacock feathers and nylon and gold and black antlers, like a crown.

Yes, she would be Carnival Queen. There couldn't be anyone in this town more regal, more befitting the honour than her, and yet Esther didn't want to pay her tribute. As she watched Jojo and his cronies, Esther saw that they didn't want to pay her tribute either. The four young men carried on with their painting and pinning as though Veronica were a passing show in which they weren't interested, while Soaky and the other designers fawned around her, adjusting this and bringing up that, layer upon layer of costume, which, when it was assembled, looked light and natural on her lithe brown body.

Now there were two reasons why Esther wanted to be in this Carnival business. There was Veronica, who was to Esther an immediate rival. Esther watched her. Ten years older, she estimated. Until a few months ago she couldn't tell anyone's age, but she knew this girl was twenty-four. She must grow up like that, Esther thought, and while doing it she must avoid some of the shortcomings of this person. Her eyebrows were shaved too thin, Esther noticed, much too thin to seem at all natural. And her voice. It was wrong. There was too much girlish excitement and high-pitchedness in it. When she was that age, her voice would have more command in it. And it would lose the suggestion of giggle which came through when Veronica pronounced herself delighted with the head-dress.

Veronica looked around and Esther saw her looking all the mas players up and down, as quickly and unnoticeably as she could. That was all right, Esther decided, standing on the periphery of the orbit of the queen. That was the way the sun should cast its light on the outer planets that turn a constant face or rotate in its light.

Then there was Jojo. There was something very deliberate about the way he wasn't impressed by the leading lady. He looked at Veronica as he would at any other brother or sister who came to put in a bit towards the task of getting their collective glory on the road. Not only that, he exchanged glances with Esther, and smiled at her. He was working on a hundred wings and she was as important to him as the woman who was undoubtedly going to be Carnival Queen.

Some of the statements that follow are true and some are false. Read them and then for each one write *true* or *false* .

1   Esther was not impressed by Veronica.
2   Veronica was not unattractive.
3   Veronica was a suitable person to be the Carnival Queen.
4   Jojo's friends pretended not to take any notice of Veronica.
5   Soaky didn't take any notice of her either.
6   Esther wasn't any good at telling people's ages.
7   She thought that when she was 24 she would be less impressive than Veronica.
8   Esther thought that Veronica should not look round at the mas players as she did.

9   Jojo didn't seem to be impressed by Veronica.
10   He did smile at Esther.

Section D   Writing

Imagine that you are either Esther or Jojo. Later on you tell a friend about seeing Veronica at the mas camp. You describe what happened and – truthfully – your feelings about it.

15 THE MODERN CITY

Section A   Planned cities

In this section ten phrases have been missed out. They are listed at the end of the section (on page 90) in the wrong order.

☐ Work out which phrase fits which space.

☐ Write the number of each space and against it write the letter of the phrase you have chosen.

In the past, most cities were not planned; they just 'happened': that is, they grew up spontaneously, with no grand design worked out for them in advance. Usually they were the natural outgrowth of villages and towns that happened to prosper. Rome started out as a small village, as did Athens, Paris, London and New York. Of course, there were exceptions to this ——— 1 ———. In ancient times, Alexander the Great planned and built seventy new cities, the most successful of which was Alexandria in Egypt, which had ——— 2

———— at its ancient peak of population. Czar Peter the Great of Russia used hundreds of thousands of convicts, peasants and prisoners-of-war to build his capital city of Saint Petersburg, now Leningrad. The capital of the United States, Washington, D.C., was also a planned city. But for the most part, cities throughout history were not the products of ———— 3 ————.

Today the reverse is true. Many nations, alarmed by the urban sprawl that has been gobbling up farmland and open countryside, and appalled by the ———— 4 ———— in the central cities, have begun building new cities that are specifically designed to meet modern needs.

Britain has long been a pioneer in planning new cities. As the first nation to become industrialized and urbanized, it faced ———— 5 ———— long before anyone else. In 1898 an Englishman, Sir Ebenezer Howard, published a book called *To-morrow: a Peaceful Path to Real Reform*, in which he advocated a new form of urban growth and organization: the 'garden city'. Such a city combined the beauty of nature – ———— 6 ———— – with all the advantages of city living, including an abundance of jobs, social and cultural centres and good shopping facilities. The garden city was to be fairly small in size and surrounded by green belts, so that the inhabitants would have ———— 7 ————, while at the same time they would be close to their work. The green belts would also serve as a 'wall', preventing the new city from spreading out too far.

In 1899 Howard organized the Garden City Association and in 1903 built the first garden city, Letchworth. It was not a very great success, but Howard still had enough faith in his idea to try again. In 1920 he started building a second demonstration model, Welwyn Garden City, which was only twenty miles northwest of London. This project, too, encountered many difficulties and failed to arouse ———— 8 ————. Nevertheless, both Welwyn and Letchworth survived and grew, and in later years – particularly after World War II – British planners looked at them with renewed interest.

The war had given the British a painful lesson in the weakness of modern, heavily populated cities. Cities were not the places of refuge they had once been. On the contrary, the invention of the aeroplane had made them the most vulnerable targets for attack. Aerial warfare made it clear that people were far safer outside ———— 9 ————. It was better not to concentrate so much of the population and industrial resources in a few large cities, but to spread them out into ————' 10 ————. Fast, modern transportation methods made such dispersal possible. Furthermore, these new towns – modelled on Howard's garden cities – could also drain off the surplus population of the large cities, relieving the overcrowded conditions, housing shortages, slums and traffic jams that plagued them.

a) easy access to the countryside
b) deliberate thought
c) staggering urban problems
d) general rule
e) many smaller towns and cities
f) nearly 1 million inhabitants
g) trees, grass, sunshine and fresh air
h) the great urban centres
i) congestion, traffic, slums and pollution
j) widespread enthusiasm

Section B   Sea city

☐ Read the passage and then answer the questions that follow it.

The floating city juts up unexpectedly from the waters of the North Sea, twenty-five miles off the coast of England. Visitors approaching by boat can see nothing but the 180-foot-high (55 metres) circular wall that surrounds the metropolis. Outside the wall lies a ring of floating cushions that deflect the waves and create a 'moat' of calm water, so that the city itself is protected from the churning seas.

The boat moves slowly through the single opening in the city wall and docks at a large harbour in the entry channel. As the passengers disembark, they see that the interior of the city resembles a huge amphitheatre, with apartment houses, shops, restaurants, theatres and power installations built on stepped terraces lining the inside of the wall. It is almost as if the 30,000 residents of Sea City were living on the broad ridges of a concrete and glass mountain that sloped gently down towards an enormous lagoon at the bottom.

Encircled by the terraced wall, the lagoon contains clusters of man-made floating islands that house offices, factories, government buildings, schools and other public facilities, as well as private homes and estates for some of the wealthier residents.

To explore the lagoon and its many islands, the visitors board electric-powered water-buses that can make round trips in just twenty-five minutes. Electricity is used instead of petroleum to avoid pollution of the lagoon, and when boats need a 'refill' they can pull up to one of many battery-charging stations.

In Sea City, the petrol station is obsolete. So is the car. Transportation along the wall terraces – connecting apartment houses with stores, clubs and restaurants – is accomplished by escalators, travelators and covered walkways.

Just like many land-based cities, Sea City is a fairly self-sufficient community. The residents work in a variety of industries, the most important of which is the exploration of undersea natural gas. But there are also several fish canneries; a boat-building plant; factories that process seaweed into fertilizer; fish farms that cultivate oysters, clams, lobsters, trout, salmon and eels; and a desalination plant where salt water is turned into fresh. Most of this water is used by Sea City itself, but the surplus is exported to arid regions throughout the world.

Supplies are brought into the floating metropolis by barge, but residents travel to and from the mainland by helibus – a vehicle that takes off and lands like a helicopter, but can also tuck in its rotors and fly like a normal aeroplane. The twenty-five-mile flight to the main-land takes fifteen minutes and costs about $1.00 or 40 pence.

There is no urgent need, however, for the residents to make frequent trips ashore, for Sea City provides them with almost all the services and amenities they could want. Most of them live in centrally heated, air-conditioned apartments on the terraced city wall. At their disposal are libraries, a 200-bed hospital, clinics, dental services, art galleries, cinemas, museums, churches, open-air tea gardens, and social centres. The central basin of the lagoon is reserved for swim-ming, sailing, water-skiing and skin-diving, while some of the wall terraces have been set aside for a football field, tennis courts, bowling greens and croquet lawns.

The marine city is small enough – 4,700 feet (1,433 metres) long by 3,300 feet (1,006 metres) wide – for people not to have to travel very far either to work or to play. And despite the fact that the whole urban island was artificially built, its clean water, fresh air and beautiful lagoon make it seem more natural and unspoiled than the polluted, congested cities on the mainland.

☐ For each of these questions choose the answer that is most suitable. Write down the letter of the answer you have chosen.

1 What shape is Sea City, seen from above?
   a)   b)

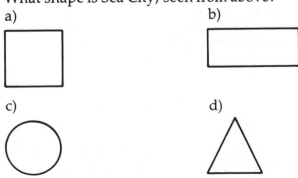

   c)   d)

2 What shape is it, seen in cross-section?

a)
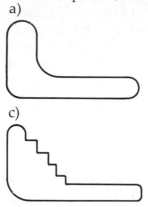

b)
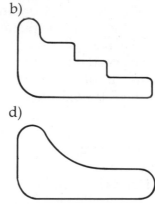

c)

d)

3 How do people travel along the wall terraces?
   a) by car
   b) by train
   c) by boat
   d) by travelator

4 Which of these industries is *not* found in Sea City?
   a) fruit canning
   b) fish farming
   c) desalination
   d) boat building

5 Which of these forms of transport is *not* used by people who live in Sea City?
   a) helibus
   b) escalator
   c) barge
   d) car

6 Which of these is a land sport available to the people of Sea City?
   a) sailing
   b) croquet
   c) cricket
   d) skiing

7 How big is Sea City?
   a) about 1000 metres by 1400 metres
   b) about 1400 metres by 1600 metres
   c) about 1100 metres by 1400 metres
   d) about 1400 metres by 100 metres

☐ Read the passage and then follow the instructions after it.

1   The tentacles of the city are not only reaching towards the sea; they are stretching upwards as well. Skyscrapers are a familiar sight in many of the world's major cities, and it is now technically possible to build them as high as 150 storeys.

2   It has been estimated that all of Chicago's business area could be housed in twelve 150-storey towers, each with 3 million square feet (280,000 square metres) of rentable area. These superstructures could easily replace the 154 major office buildings that are now spread throughout the downtown area, leaving ample room for housing, parks and gardens in the heart of Chicago's business section.

3   The city already has some of the world's tallest buildings, including 'Big John' – the 100-storey John Hancock Building that contains 705 residential apartments in addition to offices. With a population of about 12,000, 'Big John' is practically a city in itself. When the building was nearing completion several years ago, the advertisements proclaimed:
Live Uptown . . . Work Downtown. You Can Commute by Elevator in Seconds.

4   People who live and work in the building – also known as 'vertical city' – have hardly any reason for venturing outside it. The first 5 floors contain banks, stockbrokers' offices and retail shops. The next 7 floors have parking spaces for thousands of cars, followed by 28 floors of office space. The 44th floor serves as a 'sky lobby', containing a drugstore, barber's shop and other small stores and services. Apartments begin on the 45th floor and go up to the 92nd. Above this are 8 floors containing restaurants, an observation deck and mechanical equipment.

5   But, as residents have found out, living in the stratosphere has certain disadvantages. A power failure that halts elevator service can imprison people in their vertical city or leave them stranded in the street. Although the views from the upper storeys are magnificent, residents cannot always tell what the weather is like because they are often above the level of the clouds. They have to make a trip downstairs to see if it is raining outside.

6   As large as it is, 'Big John' is about to be dwarfed by the new Sears Building in Chicago that will rise 110 storeys and provide floor space equal to sixteen city blocks. At 1,450 feet (442 metres), the Sears building will be the world's tallest skyscraper, edging out New York City's 110-storey World Trade Center by just 100 feet (31 metres).

7   Despite the protests of critics who complain that the steel and glass giants are ugly and dehumanizing, more skyscrapers are springing up in every city where land is costly and scarce. It is hard to match the economic benefits of building upwards. The Sears building, for example, takes up just one acre (4,047 square metres) of ground space while providing offices for 16,500 persons. (Another two acres, however, are being used for a plaza surrounding the building.)

8   Skyscrapers have also invaded the major cities of Europe, Asia and Latin America, although not in large numbers as yet. Sometimes these new buildings have touched off angry battles between those who want to preserve the grace and harmony of the older architecture and those who claim that the new superstructures are necessary to cope with the swelling population and business boom. In London, controversy flared over the construction of a 36-storey tower on the southern edge of Hyde Park, drastically altering the neighbourhood. Similarly, many Parisians were furious about the complex of offices and apartment buildings that went up over the tracks of the old Montparnasse railroad station. One of these buildings soared 60 storeys, creating the biggest change in the low Paris skyline since the construction of the Eiffel Tower in 1889.

9   On the outskirts of Paris, a whole 'satellite city' of high-rise offices and apartments is now under construction. The complex – called the Quartier de la Défense – is intended to serve as a new urban centre that will lure many businesses and industries. Begun in 1958, the $1,000,000,000 project covers 2,000 acres (810 hectares) and is scheduled for completion in 1978. It will contain twenty-five office towers, apartments for 50,000 people, an exhibition hall, a shopping centre, theatres, restaurants and underground parking for 25,000 cars.

10   It is hoped that the new complex will relieve some of the congestion in central Paris, where traffic has become so heavy in rush hours that buses crawl along at five miles an hour – the same speed as horsedrawn carriages.

1   Copy this table and fill in the spaces:

	Big John	Sears Building	World Trade Centre
height	*not given*		
number of stories			
people housed			*not given*

2   Make a list of all the information about Big John contained in paragraphs 3 and 4. Begin like this:
    100 storeys
    750 residential apartments
    etc
3   Paragraph 5 lists some of the disadvantages of living in a skyscraper. What are they?
4   Paragraphs 8, 9, and 10 mention other places, apart from Chicago and New York, where there are skyscrapers. Make a list of them.
5   Paragraph 8 describes some of the objections to skyscrapers. Write one or two sentences expressing these in your own words.
6   Explain in your own words the effect that the Quartier de la Défense was expected to have on Paris traffic.
7   There are arguments for and against skyscrapers. Some of them are given in the passage. You can probably think of others for yourself. Some apply to people who have to live in these buildings, some apply to the other residents of the city and outsiders. Make lists of *all* the advantages and disadvantages that you can find in the passage or can think of for yourself.

Section D   Writing

Write short accounts of a typical day:
a)   as written by an inhabitant of Sea City
b)   as written by someone living at the top of Big John.

16 THE AUDITION

Section A   The great day

☐ The story that follows is taken from a longer novel. As you read the first part, ask yourself these questions:

1 Who is the narrator ('I')?
2 What is the purpose of the audition?
3 What is she going to do for her audition?
4 Who is Brandon?

The day of the *Lassie* audition arrived and my mother came into Manhattan to meet me after school and go to the studio with me on Forty-seventh Street. She was carrying a Bloomingdale's shopping bag with my costume and a tape of *Slaughter on Tenth Avenue*. 'Are you nervous?' she asked.

'Very,' I confessed.

'You're getting jitters, stage fright. That's very normal. I read somewhere that a world-famous cellist once went and hid under a table before he had to play a concert and he had been in the business over thirty years. You simply have to learn to cope with stage fright in this business. Use it. It will make you give a better performance,' she instructed.

'What if they don't like me?' I said, rejected already.

'Of course they'll like you, honey. You just relax and you'll win them over. Remember to really go for the elevation when you do those flip-flops at the end.'

'I will, Mom,' I said.

She was so excited, it was hard to believe she was so sick!

We opened the door to the studio and gave my name to the girl at the reception desk. She checked my name off a long list and we were shown into a large room.

'You can change in here,' one of the assistants told me, 'then wait for your name to be called.'

'I'll meet you back here,' my mother told me. 'I'll try to see what the competition is.'

I changed real fast. I was getting very, *very* nervous. When I had finished getting into the somewhat dazzling sequined costume my mother had made me, I joined her and the other kids and mothers in the main waiting room. I saw two girls from my school. One was Rosalind Urbell, a girl I had never particularly liked. She was very snooty and acted as though she was already a star. She was dressed in a purple costume with fringe that was even louder than mine. The other girl was someone whose name I couldn't remember, but she was in my biology class. I thought she was too heavy to be a dancer. I thought she might be something like a teenage comedienne or have a talent for playing the piano. All the mothers and kids were trying to look very cool and collected as they waited, but the tension was enough to ignite a hydrogen bomb. I decided the only way I could get through it was to think of Brandon. Wouldn't he be thrilled if I got the part he had told me about that first night he called? And then I remembered him reaching toward me, bringing me to him for our first kiss on his secret island. He would come back soon. He *had* to.

I had already crossed off eight weeks on my calendar. That meant three weeks to Christmas, when I just felt he'd be home. What could I do to make three weeks go by fast? I could keep busy every minute. Take a lot of classes, shop for some clothes and get my hair trimmed. Then I would be ready at any moment for Brandon to come home and surprise me. Surely he'd be home for Christmas. I felt like something new and crisp. Maybe cut my hair shorter. Get rid of the bangs I had had since I was born. Maybe I wasn't ready to get rid of those, but . . .

Writing

Suppose that this passage formed one episode from a magazine serial. Write a short introduction (50–100 words) explaining the situation so that new readers will understand what is going on. If there are details which you need but do not know, make them up. If you do so, make sure that they fit in with the part of the story that you have read.

Section B My turn

Eight sentences have been missed out from this section. They are listed – in the wrong order – at the end.

- [ ] Read the passage and work out which sentence fits in which space.
- [ ] Write the number of each space and the letter of the sentence you think should fill it.

The increased nervous chatter brought me back to reality. ———— 1 ————
A man started walking past me toward the tape recorder with a pile of tapes. The producers were sitting right in front of a stage area and there were several men in a sound booth; there was also a photographer taking a lot of pictures, which was unusual for any ordinary audition. Some of the girls *sang* and danced; many just danced. Three girls had picked exactly the same audition song, and one girl did an elaborate mime to *I Enjoy Being a Girl*. I wondered how so many girls had shown up and where all those mothers had come from. ———— 2 ———— Was it always someone's mother or father who had caught the bug and passed it on to their kids? I kept watching Rosalind Urbell and she did nothing but play with her fringe, which made me even more nervous. When Rosalind did her routine, it seemed to consist of nothing but twirling – she kept spinning around and kicking out her legs to the tune of *Hey, Look Me Over*.
———— 3 ———— Actually, it was my mother who heard it called and tapped me on my arm. I was still dreaming of Brandon, of his head on my lap, stretching, humming as I smoothed his beautiful hair.
'It's you,' she said.
———— 4 ————
'Good luck,' my mother whispered.

As I started running up toward the stage area, I forgot how my dance began. As a matter of fact, I forgot all the steps. My hands had gotten ice cold. My heart was jumping a mile a minute and I wanted to run out of the room!

———— 5 ———— Have courage.

I made it to the stage and looked around. To me, the stage always became a test and I was terrified of failing. I didn't want to disappoint my mother and I wanted the producers to like me.

———— 6 ———— I looked out at the people in the room. I could hear my mother whispering, 'Gather yourself,' and so I closed my eyes for a fraction of a second to find the centre of me, as she would say. I could hear her voice, 'Find the centre, the centre.' The music started and after the first moment, it all came back to me. I stopped thinking and just let my body take over, one step leading to the next, just as I had rehearsed it over and over again the last few months.

———— 7 ———— It was almost over and I'd be finished. I couldn't forget about all the people sitting out there, about all the judging, about Rosalind Urbell's fringes and my mother and father. I couldn't wait for the last ten bars; then before I knew it the music built to a crescendo and I landed in a split. Four minutes of dancing felt like an hour onstage, and was I relieved that it was over. ———— 8 ———— I went back to my seat knowing that I had done the best I could. My mother seemed pleased, too, which made me feel wonderful.

a)   'Oh, God,' was all I could muster.
b)   Why did everybody want to get into show business?
c)   Then there was silence.
d)   Finally, I heard my name called.
e)   The audience applauded and smiled.
f)   I licked my lips to make them glisten.
g)   Then as the music builds in *Slaughter*, I became aware I was halfway through.
h)   Have courage, I started saying to myself.

Section C   The winner

This section is divided into ten parts. Except for the first part, these have been printed in the wrong order.

☐ Read them through and work out the correct order. Write the numbers in that order.

Now we just had to wait until the end, when the judges would announce the winner. That was the hardest part of all, the part I couldn't prepare for.

There were seven more girls after me and then the producers got into a huddle in the corner for several minutes of consultation.

1   'However,' he said, 'the difficult part has been selecting the winner.'

All I wanted was for someone to let me out of this suspense, and a glass of water because my throat was dry. The next moment could make the difference between anonymity and a new streak of fortune. Looking over to my mother, I could see the hopeful anticipation in her eyes as she sat forward in her seat waiting for my name to ring out in the auditorium.

2   It wasn't my name he said. It wasn't *me*. I sat there dumbfounded a moment, trying to digest the news. I think this is what you call shock. All I said to myself was *Don't cry. Don't let my eyes give away the disappointment and rejection I am feeling at this moment.*

3   I'm sure every one of the girls thought it was herself.

'This girl shows signs of being a great performer. The winner is
. . .'

There was complete silence.

'. . . Rosalind Urbell,' he said with great animation.

'Rosalind Urbell,' I said to myself, incredulously.

4   Now I knew.

Various sounds broke out in the room, from astonishment to hushed disagreement, as everyone hid her disappointment and applauded the winner. Rosalind went up onstage to receive her congratulations from the producers.

'Don't worry about it – you can't win them all,' my mother said consolingly.

5   My mother had burst into tears and she was openly crying, her arm covering her eyes. She never knew I had seen her.

6   A part of me was afraid to wish I had won. I had danced the best I could. The question was: Had they picked me as winner?

'With much difficulty and deliberation,' the producer continued in a very professional-sounding monotone, 'we have selected a young girl who has a great deal of charm and talent.'

7 Finally a distinguished-looking man got up on the stage and everyone sat absolutely still. This producer said that this had been a
promotional audition to arouse local interest in the show. Then he
went on about being very pleased and appreciative of all the fabulous
participation by the young people and all the support from their
parents.

8 'We'll just move on to the next one.'
   'Right, Mom,' I said, grabbing my Bloomingdale's shopping bag
and starting up to the dressing room to change out of my costume.
'I'm sorry.'
   'Don't worry,' Mom said. 'The next one, that'll be the big one.'
   As I went off, I looked back.

9 To do this, I kept my eyes focused on an empty spool of tape. That
helped hold back the tears. Then I exhaled and felt a tremendous
relief. Win or lose, the months of pressure that had built up were
over. Tonight I could go to sleep without worrying whether I'd win
the audition or not.

Section D   Writing

Imagine that you are Rosalind Urbell. Tell the story from her point of
view.

What happens next?

While we are reading stories we often have a guess about what will happen next. In this section that is what you will be asked to do. It contains four stories. Each one is divided into parts. After each part there are questions asking you to guess what you think will happen in the next part. So that people are not tempted to cheat, all the parts are jumbled up and numbered. You will be told the number of the part you have to read.

The Primitives

How quickly things could get out of hand, how difficult it could be to say to yourself, 'No, Greg, no. No farther.' But you didn't say it and you were in it up to the eyes. Yet perhaps he wouldn't have gone back if it hadn't been for Peggy.

It would have been easy enough to have slunk up to the house, easy enough to have let it slide because he'd be heading for home in another day. They wouldn't have been able to touch him, wouldn't have come knocking at the door or anything. There was nothing they could have done and he didn't give two hoots for any of them, except her. Of course he didn't know that they had urged her to follow him and that her smile when she had caught up was a fraud.

'Go on, Peggy,' Bill had urged (her brother, the big one, nearly fifteen), 'go after him, egg him on, he's real sweet on you. He'll string himself up like a chicken and this we've gotta see, unless he funks it, and he wouldn't dare.' So Greg took the coil of rope from the shed and hurried back through the wind-shaken fronds of the aniseed, down to the creek again, and Aunt Paula, he hoped, had no idea that he had been near the house or had gone.

a) *What was going on here?*
b) *Whose thoughts are we reading?*
c) *Who were the other people?*
d) *What were they like?*
e) *What was the situation?*
f) *What was the rope for?*

Sister Coxall's Revenge

Sister Coxall had been in Violet Ward for many years. Her pride and joy was her own little office, scrupulously clean, its walls glistening with fresh white paint. A bowl of crisp daffodils stood on the middle of her desk exactly an inch away from the leather bound blotter. The arrangement of pens behind the blotter gave the impression of rigor mortis soldiers all in a row, their black caps tightly screwed on.

Sister Coxall sat at her desk, her eyes unseeing. She pondered deeply. Who was this new doctor, anyway? Some silly youth fresh from medical school? What right had he to interfere in the running of her ward? Her small hand tightened into a fist. What right had he to even voice an opinion?

a)   *What impression do you get of Sister Coxall's personality?*
b)   *What do you think she looked like?*
c)   *How did she feel at the beginning of the story?*

3 | Next Door

The old house was divided into two dwellings by a thin wall that passed on, with high fidelity, sounds on either side. On the north side were the Leonards. On the south side were the Hargers.

The Leonards – husband, wife, and eight-year-old son – had just moved in. And, aware of the wall, they kept their voices down as they argued in a friendly way as to whether or not the boy, Paul, was old enough to be left alone for the evening.

'Shhhhh!' said Paul's father.

'Was I shouting?' said his mother. 'I was talking in a perfectly normal tone.'

'If I could hear Harger pulling a cork, he can certainly hear you,' said his father.

'I didn't say anything I'd be ashamed to have anybody hear,' said Mrs Leonard.

'You called Paul a baby,' said Mr Leonard. 'That certainly embarrasses Paul – and it embarrasses me.'

'It's just a way of talking,' she said.

'It's a way we've got to stop,' he said. 'And we can stop treating him like a baby, too – *tonight*. We simply shake his hand, walk out, and go to the movie.' He turned to Paul. 'You're not afraid – are you boy?'

'I'll be all right,' said Paul. He was very tall for his age, and thin, and had a soft, sleepy, radiant sweetness engendered by his mother. 'I'm fine.'

'Damn right!' said his father, clouting him on the back. 'It'll be an adventure.'

'I'd feel better about this adventure, if we could get a sitter,' said his mother.

'If it's going to spoil the picture for you,' said his father, 'let's take him with us.'

Mrs Leonard was shocked. 'Oh – it isn't for children.'

'I don't care,' said Paul amiably. The why of their not wanting him to see certain movies, certain magazines, certain books, certain television shows was a mystery he respected – even relished a little.

'It wouldn't kill him to see it,' said his father.

'You *know* what it's about,' she said.

'What *is* it about?' said Paul innocently.

Mrs Leonard looked to her husband for help, and got none. 'It's about a girl who chooses her friends unwisely,' she said.

'Oh,' said Paul. 'That doesn't sound very interesting.'

'Are we going, or aren't we?' said Mr Leonard impatiently. 'The show starts in ten minutes.'

Mrs Leonard bit her lip. 'All right!' she said bravely. 'You lock the windows and the back door, and I'll write down the telephone numbers for the police and the fire department and the theatre and Dr Failey.' She turned to Paul. 'You *can* dial, can't you, dear?'

'He's been dialing for years!' cried Mr Leonard.

'Ssssssh!' said Mrs Leonard.

'Sorry,' Mr Leonard bowed to the wall. 'My apologies.'

'Paul, dear,' said Mrs Leonard, 'what are you going to do while we're gone?'

'Oh – look through my microscope, I guess,' said Paul.

'You're not going to be looking at germs, are you?' she said.

'Nope – just hair, sugar, pepper, stuff like that,' said Paul.

His mother frowned judiciously. 'I think that would be all right, don't you?' she said to Mr Leonard.

'Fine!' said Mr Leonard. 'Just as long as the pepper doesn't make him sneeze!'

'I'll be careful,' said Paul.

Mr Leonard winced. 'Shhhhh!' he said.

a) *What do you think of the way Mr and Mrs Leonard treated Paul?*

b) *How do you imagine Paul felt about it?*

4 | The Day After The End of The World

The radio was the first indication that anything was wrong. Right in the middle of Terry Wogan, on a Friday morning, it went dead. No fuss or bother, just silence. Ken gave his tranny a dirty look over the rim of his teacup and hit it with the flat of his hand, but it stayed dead. He took the back off and poked it with a knife, but failed even to raise a crackle of static. Touching the terminals of the battery to his tongue made him see sparks, so it wasn't that. He sat looking at the gutted corpse of his radio and chewed absently on a piece of cold toast. A radio wasn't something he could fix, so it meant a ten-mile ride to the village to get it seen to. Ken looked up at the window, scoured with rain, and frowned. Tomorrow maybe.

Outside, the rain lashed and dimmed the hills. He stood at the window sipping his tea and watching the rain stipple the loch's surface, and scratched meditatively at the beard he was trying to grow.

In the living room, he lit the gas fire and stood at the big window while the room warmed up, then he sat down at the typewriter and wrote for the rest of the day. In the early evening he tried to phone his publisher, but the lines must have been down again because the instrument was dead.

Force of habit made him turn the radio on when he sat down for breakfast the next day, and he swore at himself for the habit when nothing happened.

That's what happens if you get too dependent on the outside world, he thought as he slapped marmalade on his toast, and he decided to leave the radio until he could come up to it seven days in a row without turning it on. That seemed like a good idea. Cut off from external stimuli he might turn out something interesting. Yes, that might turn out to be an interesting experiment.

The phone was still dead, but that happened a great deal. It didn't worry him much; considering the line they'd had to lay to reach him, and considering the state of Eilbeag's little exchange, he was lucky to be able to get through anywhere at all. He'd worked it out once, and it came out that the phone was out of action a whole month in every twelve. Reasons ran from lightning to lack of staff on the exchange, and he'd learned to live with it. Down in the valley, Eilbeag was prone to flooding after heavy rain, and that got into the cable conduit which supplied power to the exchange, and that killed phone traffic. He put the phone back on its cradle and frowned. Not a sound; not even random static. His line must be down. He'd tell them when he went down with the radio – no, that was seven days away at least. Never mind, he decided as he sat down at the typewriter for chapter twelve. He could do without the phone as well.

a) *Where do you think Ken was living?*
b) *What kind of person was he?*
c) *Can you think of anything that might have caused the radio and the telephone to fail at the same time?*

5   The wrench seemed to come from nowhere, the sudden wrench that spilled spray from the rope across the water. It was Peggy at the end of it, seen starkly, wrenching, and tearing him out of the tree, twigs and leaves and rough-edged bark and the horrible yellow dam, oceans of it, crashing round him, opaque and dark, filling his mouth and eyes. He came up kicking and spitting and splashing, barely able to see, but the bottom was there, soft, slushy ooze about four feet down. He tried to spit his mouth clean, tried to shake his vision clear, and felt his feet sinking into that horrible sucking ooze, a ghastly terrifying sensation, like being swallowed alive. That crazy girl, that crazy fool. 'Help me, will ya',' he screamed.

Was it possible the kids hadn't moved, that they were still standing round like stunned ducks? And that flurry in the middle of the dam, that disordered head of hair coming his way, was it *her*?

He fought to drag his feet up with a frantic kind of strength, outraged, and broke free and floundered up the bank slipping and slithering, punching at the kids who came near.

'Greg!'

But he ran from her voice.

'Greg!'

He blundered into the bush not caring which way he went or where.

'Greg! Don't run away!'

He found himself groaning against a tree and saw her through a giddy sort of swirl. She was drenched, a horrible looking mess, a beautiful mess, and he moaned, 'You rotten girl.'

There are a few sentences left in the story. They describe how Peggy and the others reacted to what had happened. What do you think that reaction was?

6

Sister Coxall listened, a faint pink flush tinged her ears. Reality bloomed in the shape of the lawn outside the window, her eyes taking in the neatness of its razor trimmed edges.

The day had arrived. She looked around her office. She was to be removed from this, her home, and cast among strangers.

'No,' she screamed, and her fist came heavily down upon the blotter, scattering the pens into sudden life.

Sister Coxall's mind began to work. Now it raced. Nobody knows he is here except me. He said he was staying at an hotel last night and would be coming straight to the ward this morning, before reporting to the General Office. He had no white coat or identity badge yet.

A diabolical smile drew back the corners of her thin straight mouth. 'There is only one thing to do,' she muttered, and rose and went to the door.

a) *What was that one thing?*
b) *What did she do when she got to the door?*

7

'Little boys' pockets!' she said, delighted. 'Full of childhood's mysteries. An enchanted frog? A magic pocket-knife from a fairy princess?' She caressed the lump.

'He's not a little boy – he's a big boy,' said Paul's father. 'And he's too old to be thinking about fairy princesses.'

Paul's mother held up her hands. 'Don't rush it, don't rush it. When I saw him asleep there, I realized all over again how dreadfully short childhood is.' She reached into the pocket and sighed wistfully. 'Little boys are so hard on clothes – especially pockets.'

She brought out the ball and held it under Paul's nose. 'Now, would you mind telling Mommy what we have here?' she said gaily.

The ball bounced like a frowzy chrysanthemum, with ones, fives, tens, twenties, and lipstick-stained Kleenex for petals. And rising from it, befuddling Paul's young mind, was the pungent musk of perfume.

Paul's father sniffed the air. 'What's that smell?' he said.

Paul's mother rolled her eyes. *'Tabu,'* she said.

This is the end of the story. Do you think it is a good place to end?
If so, why?
If not, how would you have ended it?

8

Standing in the doorway, leaning against the frame, was a man in a spacesuit. It was white, with white helmet and dark visor and backpack. The figure was dragging its left leg, and the fabric was torn and bloody at the left knee.

The figure moved, and broke the spell. It was too tall, suspiciously slim. Ken lifted the gun. 'Careful!'

The figure touched a box attached to its belt. Ken noticed tools hanging from loops. Any one of them could have been a weapon. And he didn't recognize any one of them.

'Help me,' said the box. 'I'm hurt.'

The English was perfect, accentless. Ken didn't let the gun waver. 'I don't know who you are, but I'll shoot if you cause any trouble.'

The figure lifed a hand. 'Don't –'

'Sit down,' Ken said, gesturing with the gun at the chair in the corner.

'I am –' the figure began to protest.

'Sit down!' Ken yelled. 'Over there!'

With one hand on the wall the figure in the suit limped over to the chair and sat down heavily, leg stuck stiffly out in front of it, gloved hands folded in its lap. The dark single eye of the helmet stared blindly at him.

Ken waved the gun. 'The helmet. Take it off.'

'Your atmosphere –'

'Take it off!'

'Suppose I won't,' the box suggested.

Ken hefted the gun. 'Yes. Suppose.'

The fingers paused, hesitated. 'Mm.' It lifted its hands to the throat of its suit, manipulated seals. Sealing rings popped open. The figure lifted its hands to its head, gave the helmet a half turn on its neck ring and lifted it off, shook free long golden hair.

A starved Giacometti sculpture carved from jet with hair of spun gold. Thin face, tight mouth, star-blue eyes. Male, Ken decided, but it was hard to tell. It couldn't be human.

a)   *Describe in your own words what the alien looked like.*
b)   *What are your first impressions of it?*
c)   *What do you think it wanted?*

9   Needing that rope was like needing food. If you were hungry you ate; if you were sick to death of being teased you got reckless, you got wild.

    Aunt Paula would have been shocked in her maidenly way, would probably have declared, 'For pity's sake, Greg; what a *primitive* response.' She was too old to understand, too cut off from the real world. 'The Robinsons and the O'Connors are such nice boys,' she had said a week ago. 'They've been so anxious for you to arrive. Counting the days, they've been.' They'd been counting them all right, *and* rubbing their hands together in glee.

    Peggy was waiting in the shade, looking terrific, looking lean and alive, as if she could leap into the air and fly. He had almost convinced himself she'd be gone, that her loyalty to the crowd would have drawn her away. Finding her there, still there, was like winning the prize after you thought you'd come last.

    'Good,' she said, 'you've got it!' And he mistook for sparkle the hard excitement in her eyes.

    'Yeh, you bet.'

    She was a terrific girl. None of his friends back home, boy or girl, had half her spirit or half her nerve. He longed to take her hand as they went away from the creek, to grow strong on her touch, but he was too shy. He had never held a girl's hand, not properly, and wasn't used to 'grown-up' ways. It was surprising, really, that country kids were more grown-up than kids in town.

    'Yeh,' he repeated, swinging the rope, 'I've got it, I'll do it, you'll see,' and gave a grin that he imagined to be tough in the manner of a man. True, he was tall for thirteen, but was panicking inside like a ten-year-old. 'Will they still be there, you reckon?'

    'They'll be there.' Her tone should have warned him; it was so plain.

    a)   *What was Greg's opinion of Peggy?*
    b)   *Was he right about her?*

10   '"I love you,"' she said bitterly, '"let's make up and start all over again."'

    'Baby,' said the man desperately, 'it's another Lemuel K. Harger. It's got to be!'

    'You want your wife back?' she said. 'All right – I won't get in her way. She can have you, Lemuel – you jewel beyond price, you.'

    '*She* must have called the station,' said the man.

'She can have you, you philandering, two-timing, two-bit Lochin-var,' she said. 'But you won't be in very good condition.'

'Charlotte – put down that gun,' said the man. 'Don't do anything you'll be sorry for.'

'That's all behind me, you worm,' she said.

There were three shots.

Paul ran out into the hall, and bumped into the woman as she burst from the Harger apartment. She was a big, blonde woman, all soft and awry, like an unmade bed.

She and Paul screamed at the same time, and then she grabbed him as he started to run.

'You want candy?' she said wildly. 'Bicycle?'

'No, thank you,' said Paul shrilly. 'Not at this time.'

'You haven't seen or heard a thing!' she said. 'You know what happens to squealers?'

'Yes!' cried Paul.

She dug into her purse, and brought out a perfumed mulch of face tissues, bobbypins and cash. 'Here!' she panted. 'It's yours! And there's more where that came from, if you keep your mouth shut.' She stuffed it into his trousers pocket.

She looked at him fiercely, then fled into the street.

Paul ran back into his apartment, jumped into bed, and pulled the covers up over his head. In the hot, dark cave of the bed, he cried because he and All-Night Sam had helped to kill a man.

A policeman came clumping into the house very soon, and he knocked on both apartment doors with his billyclub.

Numb, Paul crept out of the hot, dark cave, and answered the door. Just as he did, the door across the hall opened, and there stood Mr Harger, haggard but whole.

'Yes, sir?' said Harger. He was a small, balding man, with a hairline moustache. 'Can I help you?'

'The neighbours heard some shots,' said the policeman.

'Really?' said Harger urbanely. He dampened his moustache with the tip of his little finger. 'How bizarre. I heard nothing.' He looked at Paul sharply. 'Have you been playing with your father's guns again, young man?'

'Oh, nossir!' said Paul, horrified.

'Where are your folks?' said the policeman to Paul.

'At the movies,' said Paul.

'You're all alone?' said the policeman.

'Yessir,' said Paul. 'It's an adventure.'

'I'm sorry I said that about the guns,' said Harger. 'I certainly would have heard any shots in this house. The walls are thin as paper, and I heard nothing.'

Paul looked at him gratefully.

'And you didn't hear any shots, either kid?' said the policeman.

Before Paul could find an answer, there was a disturbance out on the street. A big motherly woman was getting out of a taxi-cab and wailing at the top of her lungs.

a) *Who was this?*
b) *What was she going to do?*

11   She had met him yesterday. He had driven into the hospital grounds and almost driven over her. There were plenty of 'Go Slow' notices within sight. Besides, almost everybody who worked at the hospital knew she walked through the grounds at that time of day.

'Are you all right?' he had said, scrambling from his car. 'I really wasn't concentrating.'

His sombre eyes, glowing with concern, rested on her uniform. He seemed embarrassed. 'Er, Sister, I'm frightfully sorry.'

She couldn't help smiling. 'That's all right, Mr –' she paused politely.

'Doctor – Doctor Green. I've just arrived, as you can see,' he grinned. I'm to take over the running of D Block.'

Sister Coxall noticeably stiffened. 'D Block?' she echoed.

a) *What impression do you get of Dr Green?*
b) *Why did Sister Coxall stiffen?*
c) *What were her thoughts?*

12.   . . . there was a bright silver flash of light, then silence.

The alien stood up and looked down at the body crumpled on its back on the kitchen floor, a tiny charred hole in the chest of its sweater. He took the weapon from the table, managed to fumble open the catch. It wasn't even loaded. He gave a little smile. Nice try.

He picked up his helmet and walked to the door, opened it and stepped out onto the grass. The thunderstorm was still bubbling into existence away over the hills. He could not have been in the cottage more than ten minutes. The air smelled of rain, touched a little with the sulphur-smell that heavy industrialization gave to rain. But they hadn't expected the place to be perfect. Still, this would be a fine, fine world once they had finished mopping up.

Slowly at first, then quicker, the limp gone now, he started to walk across the grass towards the loch and the great white thing floating there.

13

The ball of money in Paul's pocket seemed to swell to the size of a watermelon. 'Yessir,' he croaked.

The policeman left.

Paul shut his apartment door, shuffled into his bedroom, and collapsed on the bed.

The next voices Paul heard came from his own side of the wall. The voices were sunny – the voices of his mother and father. His mother was singing a nursery rhyme and his father was undressing him.

'Diddle-diddle-dumpling, my son John,' piped his mother, 'Went to bed with his stockings on. One shoe off, and one shoe on – diddle-diddle-dumpling, my son John.'

Paul opened his eyes.

'Hi, big boy,' said his father, 'you went to sleep with all your clothes on.'

'How's my little adventurer?' said his mother.

'O.K.,' said Paul sleepily. 'How was the show?'

'It wasn't for children, honey,' said his mother. 'You would have liked the short subject, though. It was all about bears – cunning little cubs.'

Paul's father handed her Paul's trousers and she shook them out, and hung them neatly on the back of a chair by the bed. She patted them smooth, and felt the ball of money in the pocket.

And then what happened?

14

He was *stupid*. Surely he knew he'd need arms like wire to swing hand over hand across the dam. For a skinny-looking kid it was a stupid thing to do. What was going to happen when the rope sagged to his weight, when the branches bent down, when the rope sagged and sagged and sagged? He'd hang like a pair of pants pegged out to dry while about fifteen kids killed themselves laughing, slinging words at him and maybe stones, until finally he'd fall from the sheer impossibility of pulling himself up to the tree on the other side. Then, if anyone was left around, if they'd not all gone, someone would have to fish him out or he'd drown.

'Peggy, it's terrific that you're on my side.'

Why couldn't he leave her alone? Making her feel bad with every second word. Thudding clumsily like a puppy at her heels.

'Is it because you like me a bit?'

'Look, Greg . . .' (It was so difficult.) 'Don't ask for reasons. Save your strength. Those kids are going to give you a hard time.'

'I don't care. I'm not scared.'

What could a girl do? 'Greg, you don't have to put on an act with me.'

'But it's not an act. Honest it's not. I do things like it all the time back home.' But his voice sounded so thin he must have been shaking from head to foot with nerves.

'I'm not a drip, Peggy. Those kids don't understand. I just don't want to strip off in that horrible dam. I can't help it. It's not that I'm scared.' (He wouldn't let go. It was like being mauled.) 'I can't help it if I don't like rabbits in traps or fish on hooks. I'm not a sissy. I'm not used to that sort of thing. Those kids are so crude about it. They're so cruel. You're not like that.'

She started running, simply to get away.

'Can't they see it hurts the fish? Haven't they heard the rabbits cry?' His feet thudded at her heels. 'You know they hurt me, too, the things they say.'

There they all were, still waiting at the dam, and breathlessly she stopped in full view, so ashamed, in a muddle that had her stammering for words.

'Of course I know it hurts, Greg; that's why I came.' (Still lies, more lies.) 'But save your breath. You're all blown out. You're going to need your breath.'

'You're the one who ran, not me. I wanted to go slow, to be with you.'

'Oh, Greg . . .' It didn't matter when she was with the crowd, it didn't matter a hang then, he was a nothing when she was with the crowd. 'Have you *got* to do it, Greg? Why?'

He gaped at her. 'Of course I've got to do it.'

'But why?'

'Because they're waiting. Because they're coming. Because I said I would.'

'Look, not even Bill could swing across there, and he's twice your size. You'll tear your hands to pieces, you'll pull your silly arms out. You'll fall. It's ten feet deep out there. You'll drown.'

a) *How do you think Greg reacted to this?*
b) *What do you think he did?*

15   He finished chapter twelve, started chapter eleven, and packed in at noon, had lunch, and went to bed. All in all, he decided, he'd had a decent morning. . . .

He wasn't sure what woke him. It was dark in the bedroom, but his watch said it was only four o'clock. He turned over on the bed and turned off the clock's alarm – it was almost an hour before he was due to be awake. He got up and opened the curtains. Clouds the colour of coal crawled west across the sky, their sculpted bellies mirrored in the surface of the loch, now dead calm in a windless silence. Ken scowled. He hated thunderstorms.

Something scrabbled against the wall outside.

Ken stepped back from the window and let the curtain fall. The scrabbling noise reached the window, and a bulky shadow traversed the curtain, haltingly, as if somehow crippled. Ken stood very still and watched the shadow move across the curtain and away, and the scrabbling moved along the wall again, towards the corner. The shadow fell on the other curtain, and Ken heard the other window rattle. His stomach suddenly went cold. It was trying to get in.

Someone down in Eilbeag had been burgled some time before, and last year a bike gang had all but taken over the little church hall. And only twenty miles away was the top security prison at Milgowrie. Ken took the shotgun out from under the bed and ran into the kitchen. In the welsh dresser were two boxes of cartridges. Both empty. Ken swore and snapped the gun shut.

The scrabbling sound had come round the corner and was moving along the wall towards the door. The rake, propped up against the wall, fell noisily; plant pots broke. Whoever it was, he was a clumsy beggar. Ken lifted the gun.

The scrabbling reached the door, stopped. The handle rattled as someone took hold of it, and the knob rotated. The lock opened, and the door began to swing inwards, slowly at first, then abruptly, so that it banged against the wall.

'Sweet Jesus,' whispered Ken.

a)   *What evidence is there to help the reader guess who or what might have been outside?*
b)   *How do you think Ken felt at this point?*
c)   *What do you think he saw?*
d)   *What do you think happened?*

16   He beat on the wall with his fist. 'Mr Harger! Stop it! he cried. 'Mrs Harger! Stop it!'

'For Ollie from Lavinia!' All-Night Sam cried back at him. 'For Ruth from Carl, who'll never forget last Tuesday! For Wilbur from Mary, who's lonesome tonight! Here's the Sauter-Finnegan Band asking, *Love, What Are You Doing to My Heart?*'

Next door, crockery smashed, filling a split second of radio silence. And then the tidal wave of music drowned everything again.

Paul stood by the wall, trembling in his helplessness. 'Mr Harger! Mrs Harger! Please!'

'Remember the number!' said All-Night Sam. 'Milton nine-three-thousand!'

a) *So what did Paul do?*
b) *With what results?*

17   'It seems odd, Matron, this is the tenth doctor who has failed to report for duty in ten years. I must say though, that Sister Coxall manages admirably, a true devotee to her work. A doctor would find very little to do on her ward, anyway.'

18   'No,' said Ken.

'Have you no compassion?' the alien barked. 'What do you call it when a wound is very badly infected?'

'Sepsis,' Ken said quietly. 'We call it sepsis.'

Ignoring the gun, Smith bent down and pulled up the torn leg of his spacesuit. Under it, all was bloody. Ken pursed his lips. Smith said, 'It's what you call a compound fracture, yes?'

Ken nodded.

'I've very nearly drugged myself to death as it is, and it's still only just bearable. Now will you help me?'

Ken looked down at the ruin of the alien's left leg, then at the cold blue eyes. He frowned and very slowly, without taking his eyes off Smith, put the gun down on the table. Smith reached across his chest, and . . .

'and . . .' what?
How do you think the story ends?

19 Something inside him turned cold, an awful thought, so cold. 'You crummy girl. You never believed I could, did you? You've been *stringing* me along. You *are* like the others. Only worse.' Then he snarled at her, 'I'm awake up to you, Peggy O'Connor. At least the other kids are honest. At least they say it out loud.'

He thrust on ahead to meet the kids, frightened and numb and wild, talking through his teeth because he knew they'd rattle if he opened his jaws. That horrible yellow dam was still there, forty feet wide. He had hoped the earth might have sprung a leak and drained it away. 'Yeh, I've got it, Bill O'Connor. You can see. You tie it over your side and I'll tie it here. You take it up good and high. You *make* it reach. You get it up there. Are you scared to climb? And make a decent knot, Bill O'Connor; you play fair.' He was not so angry that he didn't know the kids were wary of his wildness, and surprised. Two of them were only eight, one of the Robinson girls was fifteen, that sly, heavy-lidded girl who usually giggled all the time. Risking his neck for them was mad, but he was doing it for Peggy, not them, still for her. He hated her. Everything was a blur.

It was Harry Smith who swam with the rope to the other side, Harry yelling, 'It's going to be short by yards.' Bill O'Connor yelling then, 'He'd have made sure of that. He'd have cut a bit off. I told you he'd funk it.'

Greg was climbing with his own end up into the tree, clumsily, slipping, getting tangled, realizing his branch was dipping over the dam. 'It'll reach. You wait till I've got it tied.' His voice was shrill. 'Then pull. It'll reach if O'Connor's not scared to climb.'

'Look here, you!' Bill O'Connor, hand on hip, standing over there under the opposite tree. 'Twice you've said that!'

'So what? It's true, isn't it? You know what bullies are, you and your sister. Fifteen to one and you're real brave.'

'You leave my sister out of it.'

'Why should I? She didn't leave herself out of it, did she? When country kids come to town we treat 'em kind.'

'Are you whining, mate? Are you getting sorry for yourself?'

'I'm not whining, O'Connor. I'm mad. I'm real mad.' He couldn't stop himself any more, didn't want to, didn't care, and the branch was swaying over the water. 'You've had a wonderful time, haven't you, you and your crummy sister and all your rotten crowd. I reckon you must feel real good, real brave, all fifteen of you.'

a) *At this point, suddenly something happened.*
b) *What do you think it was, and who did it?*

20 'Nurse,' she shrilled, 'a new patient is expected this morning, a Mr Green. When he arrives, bring him straight to my office.' She looked down at an empty report paper she held in her hand. 'It says here that he is paranoid and greatly deluded; he thinks he is a doctor. Humour him, Nurse. I'll prepare a strong sedative.'

Going to the cupboard, Sister Coxall took down a syringe and filled it with a cool amber liquid. She then took an empty file from a cabinet and began to prepare a written report on Mr Green.

She sighed. The ward was full of sedated men, all deluded, all insisting in their nightmare ravings that they were doctors. No one would ever take her ward and office away from her. No one.

Later that day in the General Office, the Hospital Secretary was speaking into the phone.

What was she saying?

---

21 The radio. . . . 'Did you affect the radio?'

'The lander does have a radar blanket,' Smith admitted. 'We didn't want to be shot down when we landed.'

'Telephone too?'

Smith nodded. 'I think it damps down electrical pulses or something; I don't know. I'm only a geologist.'

'You speak very good English, for a geologist.'

'And Russian, Chinese, Icelandic and a number of central European languages. Your planet radiates like a radio galaxy. We all speak at least two of your languages, just in case we have to talk to you.'

There was a hiss of static from the helmet, on the floor beside Smith's chair, then an electronic beep and a gabble of words in a liquid, quiet language. Ken jerked, just barely resisted the urge to pull the trigger. Smith pursed his lips and looked down at the helmet.

The message stopped, there was a burst of static, then the message repeated. Ken watched the helmet until the message ended, then waved the gun at Smith. 'What was that?' he said.

Smith looked uncooperative. 'I don't –'

'What did it say!' he yelled.

'I'm being called back to the lander. They'll keep repeating it at twenty-minute intervals until I respond.'

'What will they do if you don't?'

'They'll come looking for me,' Smith said softly.

'They won't be able to find you.'

'I'm carrying a beacon.'

Ken felt his stomach ice over again. 'What?'

Smith very slowly unhooked a little box from his belt. It was dented on one side, and it rattled when he shook it. 'It's broken,' he said. 'But they know which direction I came in, and they'll look for the nearest habitation.'

His arms hurt from holding the gun. 'If you're lying to me. . . .'

The alien pulled a face. 'Oh, give over. You may shoot me, but if they turn on the lander's gee fields anywhere near here they'll turn your nervous system inside out.'

'You're in no position to threaten me.'

'I'm in a better position to threaten you than you are to threaten me. Go on, shoot me with that ridiculous antique. I promise you, we tend towards the vindictive.'

Bluff with bluff. 'You don't want to die any more than I do.'

Smith smiled. 'True. I was just warning you of the consequences.'

Ken frowned, conscious that the alien was beginning to rattle him. He was going to have to think of something to do with him sooner or later.

'Look,' Smith said reasonably, shifting and stopping as Ken lifted the gun. 'I am in considerable pain. I need medical attention.'

How do you think that Ken reacted to this request?

22

Dazed, Paul went to the phone and dialled the number.

'WJCD,' said the switchboard operator.

'Would you kindly connect me with All-Night Sam?' said Paul.

'Hello!' said All-Night Sam. He was eating, talking with a full mouth. In the background, Paul could hear sweet, bleating music, the original of what was rending the radio next door.

'I wonder if I might make a dedication,' said Paul.

'Dunno why not,' said Sam. 'Ever belong to any organization listed as subversive by the Attorney General's office?'

Paul thought a moment. 'Nossir – I don't think so, sir,' he said.

'Shoot,' said Sam.

'From Mr Lemuel K. Harger to Mrs Harger,' said Paul.

'What's the message?' said Sam.

'I love you,' said Paul. 'Let's make up and start all over again.'

The woman's voice was so shrill with passion that it cut through the din of the radio, and even Sam heard it.

'Kid – are you in trouble?' said Sam. 'Your folks fighting?'

Paul was afraid that Sam would hang up on him if he found out that Paul wasn't a blood relative of the Hargers. 'Yessir,' he said.

'And you're trying to pull 'em back together again with this dedication?' said Sam.

'Yessir,' said Paul.

Sam became very emotional. 'O.K., kid,' he said hoarsely, 'I'll give it everything I've got. Maybe it'll work. I once saved a guy from shooting himself the same way.'

'How did you do that?' said Paul fascinated.

'He called up and said he was gonna blow his brains out,' said Sam, 'and I played *The Bluebird of Happiness*.' He hung up.

Paul dropped the telephone into its cradle. The music stopped, and Paul's hair stood on end. For the first time, the fantastic speed of modern communications was real to him, and he was appalled.

'Folks!' said Sam, 'I guess everybody stops and wonders sometimes what the heck he thinks he's doin' with the life the good Lord gave him! It may seem funny to you folks, because I always keep up a cheerful front, no matter how I feel inside, that I wonder sometimes, too! And then, just like some angel was trying to tell me, "Keep going, Sam, keep going,' something like this comes along.

'Folks!' said Sam, 'I've been asked to bring a man and his wife back together again through the miracle of radio! I guess there's no sense in kidding ourselves about marriage! It isn't any bowl of cherries! There's ups and downs, and sometimes folks don't see how they can go on!'

Paul was impressed with the wisdom and authority of Sam. Having the radio turned up high made sense now, for Sam was speaking like the right-hand man of God.

When Sam paused for effect, all was still next door. Already the miracle was working.

'Now,' said Sam, 'a guy in my business has to be half musician, half philosopher, half psychiatrist, and half electrical engineer! And! If I've learned one thing from working with all you wonderful people out there, it's this: if folks would swallow their self-respect and pride, there wouldn't be any more divorces!'

There were affectionate cooings from next door. A lump grew in Paul's throat as he thought about the beautiful thing he and Sam were bringing to pass.

'Folks!' said Sam, 'that's all I'm gonna say about love and marriage! That's all anybody needs to know! And now, for Mrs Lemuel K. Harger, from Mr Harger – I love you! Let's make up and start all over again!' Sam choked up. 'Here's Eartha Kitt, and *Somebody Bad Stole De Wedding Bell!*'

The radio next door went off.

The world lay still.

A purple emotion flooded Paul's being. Childhood dropped away, and he hung, dizzy on the brink of life, rich, violent, rewarding.

There was movement next door – slow, foot-dragging movement.

'So,' said the woman.

'Charlotte –' said the man uneasily. 'Honey – I swear.'

a) *What had gone wrong to make the man 'uneasy'?*

b) *What happened next?*

23

The shrug she gave was not the answer he hoped for. 'I don't write letters much.'

'Can I write to you?'

'Can't stop you, can I? I don't care.'

She was hurrying, legging through a fence and leaping over tussocks, flowing along a yard or two ahead with beautiful movements, but the faster he went the faster she went, too. It was her face he wanted to see; or was she too shy to meet him in the eye?

'I can't believe you're on my side, Peggy. I'll do it. I will, I will.'

'Of course you will. I believe you. You don't have to convince me, I told you that before. *They're* the ones you've got to show.'

'I'll not be doing it for them.'

His meaning made her shiver, but a girl couldn't wave a flag for every kid who came around. He was wet. He was limp. Too good for real. Like his aunt. 'He writes beautiful poems,' she had said. 'He'll be famous one day.' Wow. And he looked it. 'You should see him,' the kids had hooted. 'Just your size, Peggy. Maybe he'll bring you flowers.'

'He'd better not try.'

a) *The next paragraph tells us Peggy's thoughts. What do you think they were?*

b) *How did she feel about his dare?*

24

'Look, get into my car and I'll drive you to the Nurses' Home. I take it you do live in?'

They sat in silence and soon were mounting the dingy staircase leading to Sister Coxall's neat room. Once inside, she took off her cape and carefully folded it into straight pleats.

'Sit down, Doctor, I'll make some tea.'

Sitting drinking the sweet tea, Doctor Green explained how he had always been interested in the work amongst mentally disturbed people and how, when he had finished his studies, he had applied for this post in one of the country's largest psychiatric hospitals. He little thought he would be accepted, but he had, and without an interview. It seemed his references and commendations were sufficient.

He told her of the great changes and new ideas he hoped to introduce on his own block. 'For instance,' he said, 'the sister on Violet Ward has been in the same ward for ten years without ever circulating around the other wards and buildings. She surely must have lost her identity to some extent, nurse and patients fusing into one large family. Her patients are growing old with her; they must be more like children to her than sick people.' He leaned forward. 'You know, Sister, a person working with the mentally ill for any length of time without a change, is in great danger of illness herself. Tomorrow, when I begin my work, I intend to move that sister to a different ward. She may not realize it at the time, but the change will do her good.'

a)   *What did Sister Coxall think and feel now?*
b)   *What did she say or do?*

25

'Is it true you write poems, Greg?' she said.
He snarled at her.
'Would you write one about me?'
'Yeh, Greg,' Bill said (Greg hadn't seen the others there), 'how *do* you write poems? The words'll never work for me.'

a)   *What is your opinion of this ending?*
b)   *Is it what you expected?*
c)   *Is it in character for these people to behave like this?*

26

'Lem! Lem, baby.'

She barged into the foyer, a suitcase bumping against her leg and tearing her stockings to shreds. She dropped the suitcase, and ran to Harger, throwing her arms around him.

'I got your message, darling,' she said, 'and I did just what All-Night Sam told me to do. I swallowed my self-respect, and here I am!'

'Rose, Rose, Rose – my little Rose,' said Harger. 'Don't ever leave me again.' They grappled with each other affectionately, and staggered into their apartment.

'Just look at this apartment!' said Mrs Harger. 'Men are just lost without women!' As she closed the door, Paul could see that she was awfully pleased with the mess.

'You *sure* you didn't hear any shots?' said the policeman to Paul.

What answer did Paul give him?

27

The alien smiled an even row of white teeth. 'How do you know which of these are tools and which are weapons?' He touched things on his belt, here and here.

'I'll shoot you if you even look as though you're pointing one at me.' To tell the truth, he didn't know what to do.

'You're suspicious.'

'I'm scared.'

The alien put his helmet down on the floor beside the chair. 'You also have the advantage.'

'Just keep that in mind when you think of doing something silly. Are you an alien?'

The alien touched his face. 'No. I got this colour under a sun-lamp.'

Ken scowled. Were aliens supposed to have a sense of humour? 'Where are you from?'

The alien pointed at the ceiling. He pursed almost fleshless lips and took his gloves off, laid them in his lap. His fingers were long and unnaturally thin, and the palms were as black as the rest of him.

The icy cold eyes blinked at him. 'Do you think I'm stupid enough to tell you where I'm from?' he asked.

Ken shrugged. 'You're stupid enough to come asking for help.'

'I do have a desperate need.'

Granted. 'Do you have a name.'

A moment's hesitation. 'Of course I do. Smith.'

'I don't believe you.'

'Take it or leave it. My name is Smith, and I'm a geologist. Would you believe me if I told you my real name?'

All right. 'What are you doing here?'

A little smile quirked up the corner of the alien's mouth. 'Examining rocks,' he said conspiratorially.

'Stop being bloody funny.'

The smile went away. 'I'm part of a scientific team. We're here to examine your wonderful world.' He didn't sound as if he meant it.

'Where are the others?'

Smith waved a vague hand. 'I've walked a long way.'

'What happened to you?'

'I fell off a rock.'

He almost laughed. 'You're joking.'

Smith looked down at his bloody, tattered knee, and gave a strained little laugh. 'So funny, isn't it,' he said.

'Have you invaded the Earth?'

'I'm in no fit state to invade anywhere.'

'All of you. Have you invaded the Earth?'

The alien looked sour. 'Don't be stupid.'

a) *So why do you think the aliens had come to earth?*
b) *Were they friendly or hostile? What evidence is there to support your view?*

28   Soon after Paul's parents left, the radio in the Harger apartment went on. It was on softly at first – so softly that Paul, looking through his microscope on the living room coffee table, couldn't make out the announcer's words. The music was frail and dissonant – unidentifiable.

Gamely, Paul tried to listen to the music rather than to the man and woman who were fighting.

Paul squinted through the eyepiece of his microscope at a bit of his hair far below, and he turned a knob to bring the hair into focus. It looked like a glistening brown eel, flecked here and there with tiny spectra where the light struck the hair just so.

There – the voices of the man and woman were getting louder

again, drowning out the radio. Paul twisted the microscope knob nervously, and the objective lens ground into the glass slide on which the hair rested.

The woman was shouting now.

Paul unscrewed the lens, and examined it for damage.

Now the man shouted back – shouted something awful, unbelievable.

Paul got a sheet of lens tissue from his bedroom, and dusted at the frosted dot on the lens, where the lens had bitten into the slide. He screwed the lens back in place.

All was quiet again next door – except for the radio.

Paul looked down into the microscope, down into the milky mist of the damaged lens.

Now the fight was beginning again – louder and louder, cruel and crazy.

Trembling, Paul sprinkled grains of salt on a fresh slide, and put it under the microscope.

The woman shouted again, a high, ragged, poisonous shout.

Paul turned the knob too hard, and the fresh slide cracked and fell in triangles to the floor. Paul stood, shaking, wanting to shout, too – to shout in terror and bewilderment. It had to stop. Whatever it was, it *had* to stop!

'If you're going to yell, turn up the radio!' the man cried.

Paul heard the clicking of the woman's heels across the floor. The radio volume swelled until the boom of the bass made Paul feel like he was trapped in a drum.

'And now!' bellowed the radio, 'for Katy and Fred! For Nancy and Bob, who thinks she's swell! For Arthur, from one who's worshipped him from afar for six weeks! Here's the old Glenn Miller Band and that all-time favourite, *Stardust!* Remember! If you have a dedication, call Milton nine-three-thousand! Ask for All-Night Sam, the record man!'

The music picked up the house and shook it.

A door slammed next door. Now someone hammered on a door.

Paul looked down into his microscope once more, looked at nothing – while a prickling sensation spread over his skin. He faced the truth: The man and woman would kill each other, if he didn't stop them.

a) *What do you think Paul did about it?*
b) *And how did they react?*

'Are you sure the rope's long enough, Greg? Doesn't look long enough to me.'

'It'll reach. The dam's not wide. You'll see.'

'It's got to reach from tree to tree. It's got to be tied. If it's short you'll look a fool.'

'It'll reach. You'll see.'

It was unbelievable that a super girl like her should have come chasing after him. 'Don't let them beat you, Greg.' He had scarcely believed his ears. 'I'm on your side. You get that rope. For a boy who can't swim it's the bravest thing I ever heard.'

After all, he was a city kid and *they* were her family and her crowd. Their differences hadn't quite come to blows, but they were incredible kids, tough and no need to pretend, as brown as summer hills, as wiry as grass, as hard as glare. They belonged and he didn't. When they baited their hooks the fish bit; when they set traps the rabbits were caught; when they plunged into that horrible yellow dam they swam like eels; when they sunned on the bank they stripped off to the raw – if the girls were not around. Natural kids with never the embarrassment of a sense of shame. The jokes they told made him want to run a mile. Aunt Paula's Sunday School class! Holy cow!

But now he was walking with Peggy, Peggy swinging along with her hair blowing and her blouse flapping over her jeans, and it was such a short way back to the dam. He was crazy, he was mad; if he broke an arm or his neck what did he prove?

What a super holiday it could have been if there had been no Robinsons, no Smiths, and no O'Connors except her. Then he'd have got round to holding her hand and everything would have been different. He'd have liked the country then. Maybe, with her, he'd have plunged gladly into the dam. There'd have been none of the anxiety of worrying about those kids, trying to dodge them but running into them at every turn. He was fair game; the greatest thing that had happened to them in years; at last a city kid to tease ragged and tear down. No kid in his right mind would have shouted – *shouted* if you please – 'I bet you I could. I do things like that all the time back home. I bet you I could cross the dam. If I had a rope you'd see.'

So he had the rope and now had to swing hand over hand through the air with that horrible yellow dam away down there, snags and all, and its ooze. It was true he couldn't swim much. No buoyancy or something; it was strange. Even the kids at home used to grin when he floundered around.

'When I go home, Peggy,' he said, hardly daring to put it into words, 'will you write to me sometimes?'

What answer do you think Peggy gave him?